JUN   2010

ED EMBERLEY'S
BIG PURPLE

DRAWING BOOK

LITTLE, BROWN & COMPANY
LB kids

HELLO! WE ARE THE "PICTURE PEOPLE" ED EMBERLEY PUT US IN THIS BOOK,
BUT NOW HE IS BUSY DOING OTHER THINGS, SO WE NEED YOUR HELP TO MAKE

Little, Brown Books for Young Readers

Hachette Book Group

237 Park Avenue, New York, NY 10017

LB kids is an imprint of Little, Brown Books for Young Readers.

The LB kids name and logo are trademarks of Hachette Book

Group, Inc.

Visit our website at www.lb-kids.com

First Revised Edition: October, 2005

Library of Congress Cataloging-in-Publication Data

Emberley, ED.

 Ed Emberley's Big Purple Drawing Book.

 Summary: Presents step-by-step instructions for drawing people,

animals, and objects using a minimum of line and cirlce combinations.

 1. Drawing -- Technique -- Juvenile Literature.

2. Purple in Art -- Juvenile Literature. [1. Drawing -- Technique]

1. Title II. Big Purple Drawing Book.

NC670.E46 741.2'6   81-3778

          AACR2

ISBN 978-0-316-78973-8

WKT

Printed in China

10 9 8 7 6 5 4 3

US "LIVE". IF YOU WOULD TAKE US OUT ONCE IN A WHILE (BY DRAWING US)
AND LET US DO THINGS WE WOULD BE MOST GRATEFUL!

CONTENTS

5- GRAPES
6- NESSYS
13- PENGUINS
14- THINGS IN THE WATER
17- PANDAS
20- HI DIDDLE DIDDLE
22- POODLES
28- 3 PENNY ANIMALS
31- THINGS PIRATICAL
32- CAPT'N BLAH!
34- FLEA BANE
35- TWIST
40- PIRATE'S PISTOL

41- TREASURE CHEST
42- PIRATE PARROT
43- PIRATE CANNON
44- SEA HAWK
    (PIRATE SHIP)
56- SHARK
60- BUGS MALONEY
61- BEE
61- FLY
62- ANT
62- CRICKET
63- SPIDER
63- GRASSHOPPER
64- SKEETER
64- CENTIPEDE
65- PRAYING MANTIS

66- SWAMP CREATURE
68- LOLITA
70- OTHER HIPPOS
72- SUB (GUPPY)
74- SUB (BARRACUDA)
76- THAT TANK
78- PICK UP TRUCKS
84- FROO
86- FROOTER
87- TRAKIR
88- NEEBORT I.C.U.
90- DRIM
91- GINSFORTWOOZELLFIMMS
92- PURPLE PUSH PIN

INSTRUCTIONS

THIS ROW SHOWS WHAT TO DRAW.

THIS ROW SHOWS WHERE TO PUT IT.

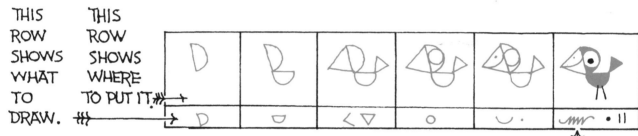

THIS SIGN MEANS "FILL IN"

THIS ALPHABET WAS USED TO MAKE ALL THE WORDS IN THIS BOOK.
ABCDEFGHIJKLMNOPQRSTUVWXYZ

THIS ALPHABET WAS USED TO MAKE ALL THE PICTURES IN THIS BOOK.
(■●▼ ∨▷C I .)

PURPLE IS A JUST-RIGHT COLOR FOR MAKING...

GRAPES

A GRAPE

GRAPE LOLLYPOP

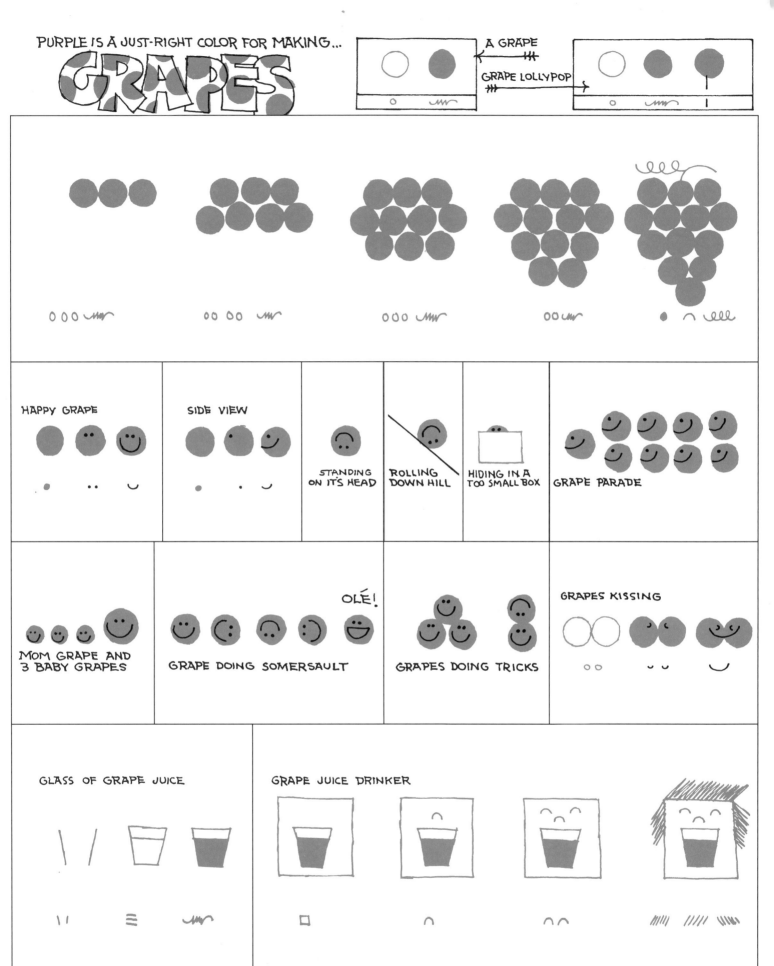

HAPPY GRAPE

SIDE VIEW

STANDING ON ITS HEAD

ROLLING DOWN HILL

HIDING IN A TOO SMALL BOX

GRAPE PARADE

MOM GRAPE AND 3 BABY GRAPES

GRAPE DOING SOMERSAULT

OLÉ!

GRAPES DOING TRICKS

GRAPES KISSING

GLASS OF GRAPE JUICE

GRAPE JUICE DRINKER

✳ OF COURSE GRAPES COME IN DIFFERENT SHAPES, SIZES AND COLORS • ALL MAKE GOOD "GRAPE PEOPLE"...

5

THE NESSYS

MRS. NESSY

MR. NESSY

MASTER NESSY

MISS NESSY

6

OTHER ASSORTED NESSYS

CAN YOU FIGURE OUT HOW I DREW THEM?

NESSY TAIL

NESSY BODY
(LOOK ABOVE TO SEE HOW IT FITS.)

A NESSY PEEKING UP
OUT OF THE WATER

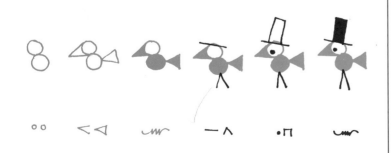

AGNES

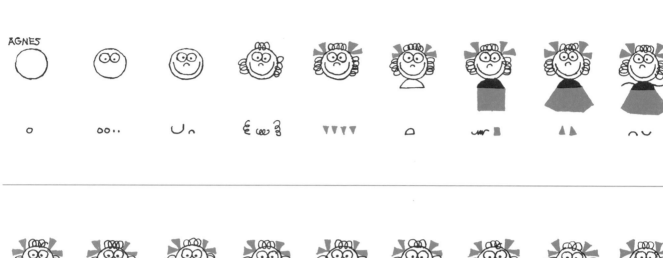

ANGUS

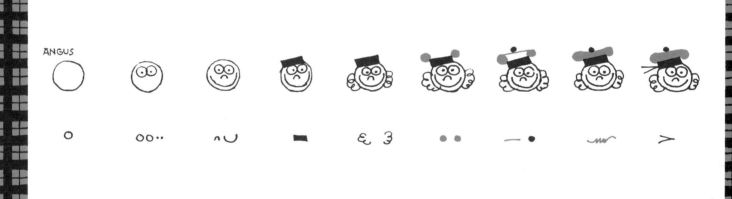

PELICAN

DUCKS

9

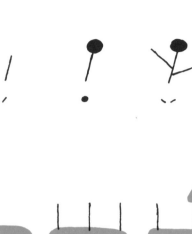

ROCKS

WITH GRASS   WITH FLOWERS

NOTICE HOW THE SAME SIZE NESSY CAN BE MADE TO LOOK BIGGER OR SMALLER, DEPENDING ON WHAT YOU PUT NEXT TO IT.

10

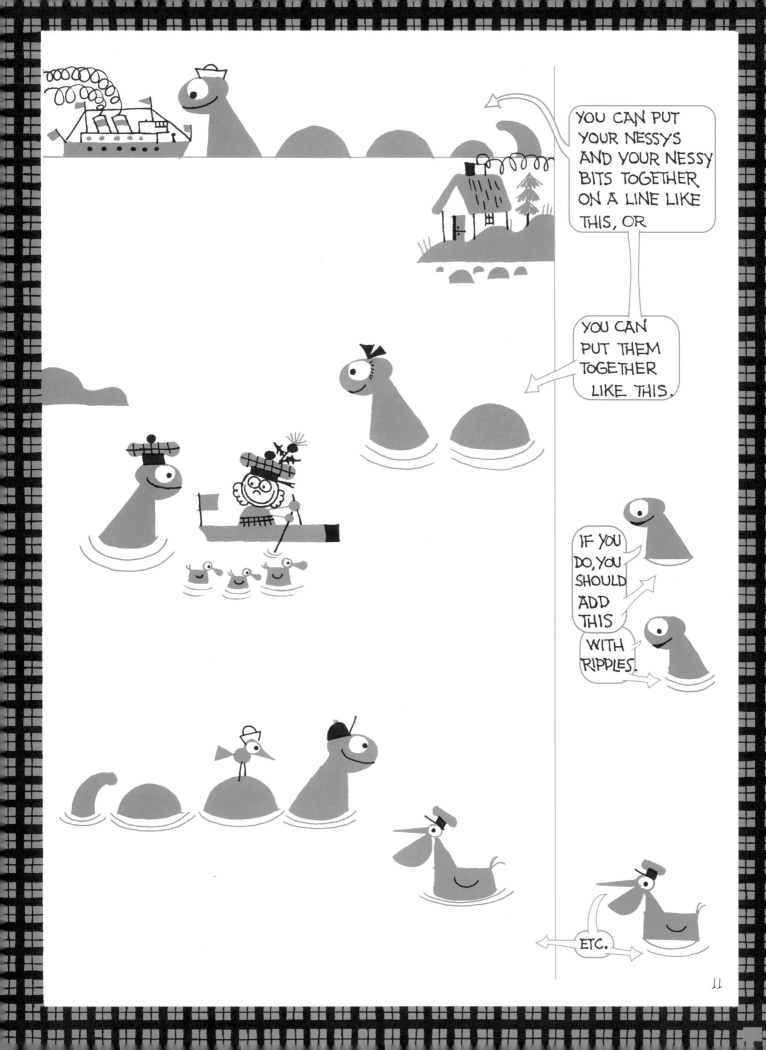

1

2

3

4

5

6

7

8

9

10

IF YOU WOULD LIKE TO ADD
UNDERWATER PARTS TO YOUR
NESSY... HERE IS ONE WAY

ETC.

PENGUINS

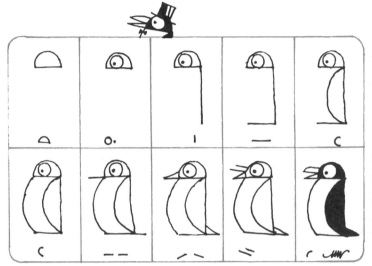

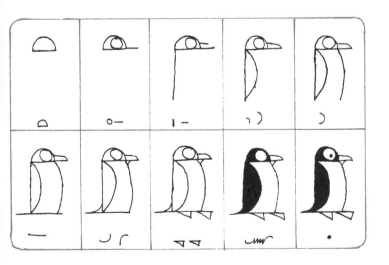

etc.

THE WATER

SHARK GOING THIS WAY ←

GOING THAT WAY →

MEAN, HUNGRY SHARK LOOKING UP.

A WHALE

SNAKE SWIMMING

FROG PEEKING UP OUT OF THE WATER

ALLIGATOR SWIMMING

SWAN SWIMMING

DOG SWIMMING (DOING THE "DOG PADDLE")

DUCK DIVING DOWN FOR FOOD

ALE'S TAIL

OTHER FROG PEEKING

SEAL IN THE WATER LOOKING AT YOU

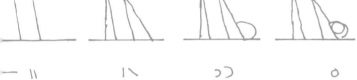

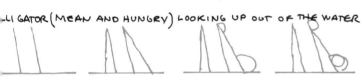

LI GATOR (MEAN AND HUNGRY) LOOKING UP OUT OF THE WATER

PENGUIN LOOKING UP OUT OF THE WATER

PENGUIN DIVING DOWN
UNDER THE WATER

DUCK SWIMMING

QUACKING

OTHER WATER ———→

ETC

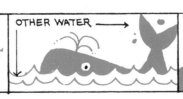

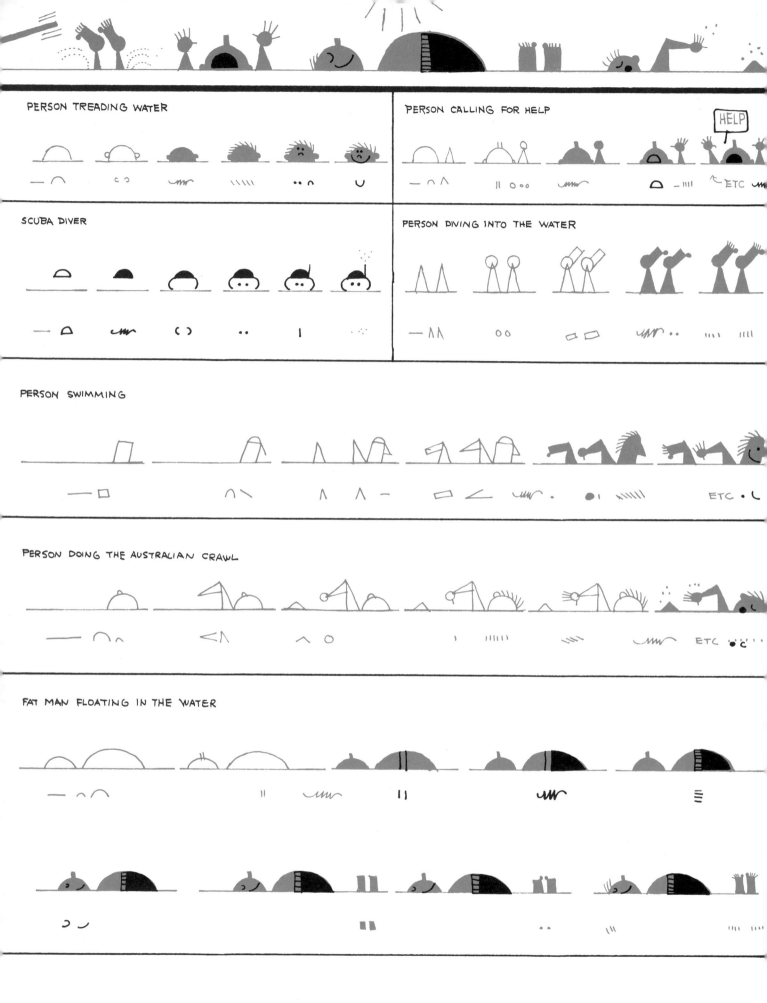

PERSON TREADING WATER

PERSON CALLING FOR HELP

HELP

SCUBA DIVER

PERSON DIVING INTO THE WATER

ETC

PERSON SWIMMING

ETC •

PERSON DOING THE AUSTRALIAN CRAWL

ETC

FAT MAN FLOATING IN THE WATER

PANDAS

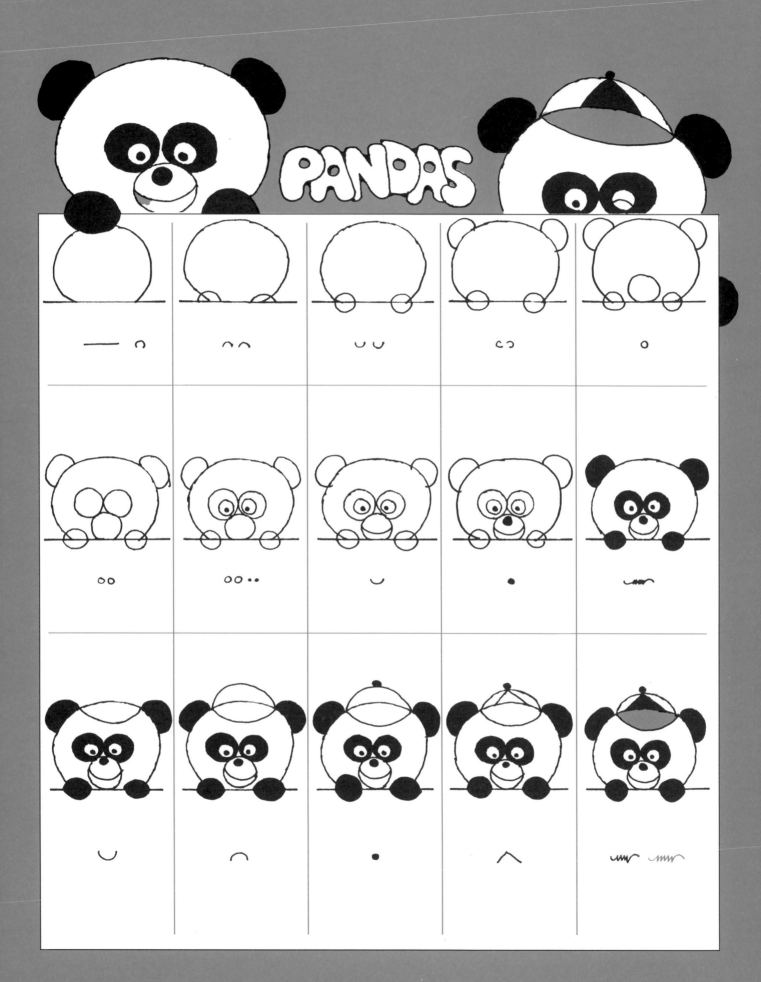

IF YOU LOOK
AT THE POODLE *
PAGES AND THE
** GINSFORTWOOZELLFIMM
PAGES YOU WILL
SEE SOME
IDEAS FOR OTHER
THINGS YOU CAN
DO WITH YOUR
PANDAS.

* POODLES, 22
** GINSFORTWOOZELLFIMMS91

18

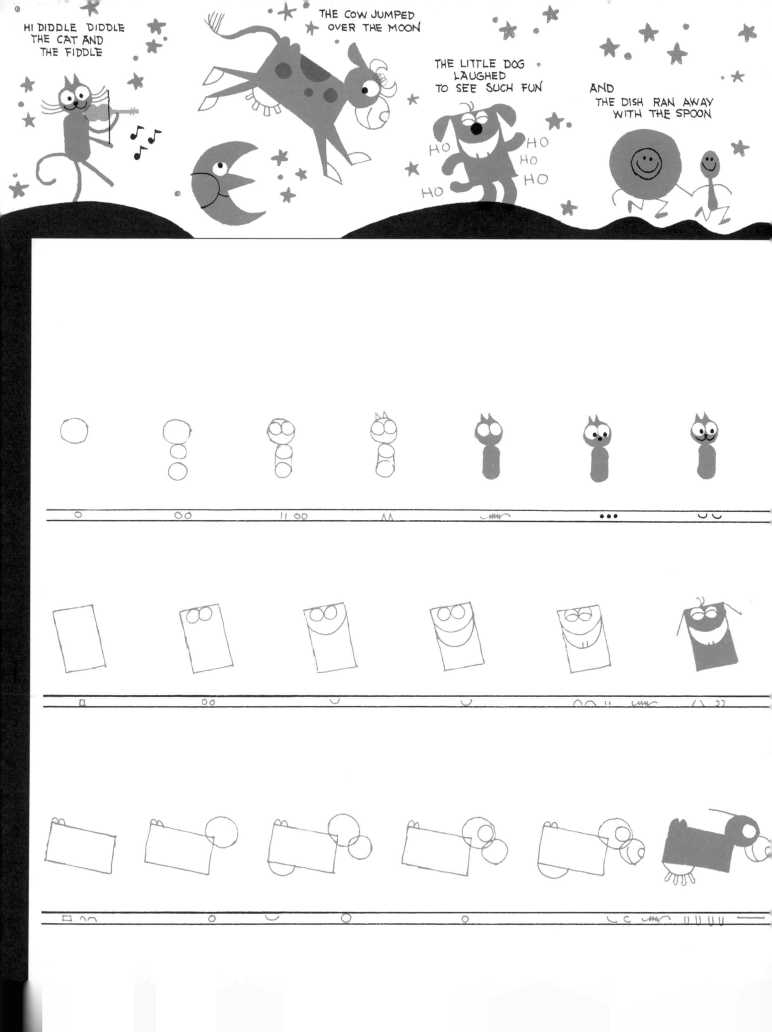

HI DIDDLE DIDDLE
THE CAT AND
THE FIDDLE

THE COW JUMPED
OVER THE MOON

THE LITTLE DOG
LAUGHED
TO SEE SUCH FUN

AND
THE DISH RAN AWAY
WITH THE SPOON

HO HO
HO
HO
HO

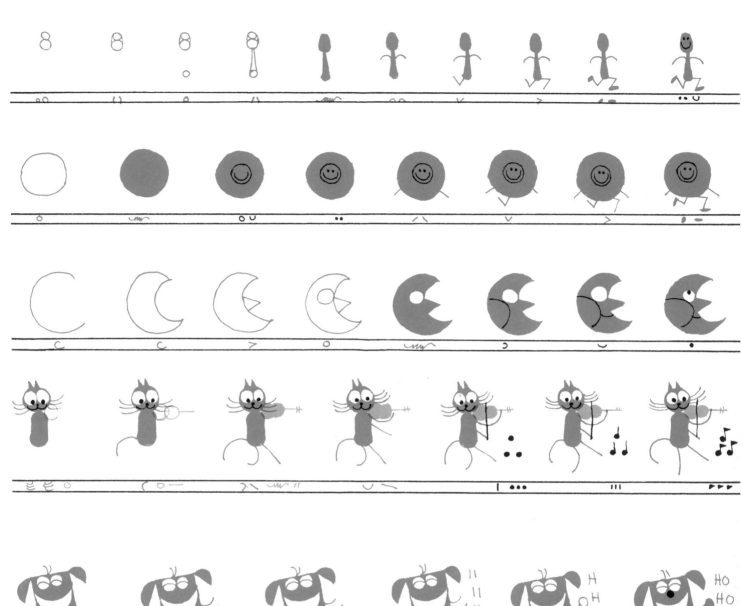

POODLES

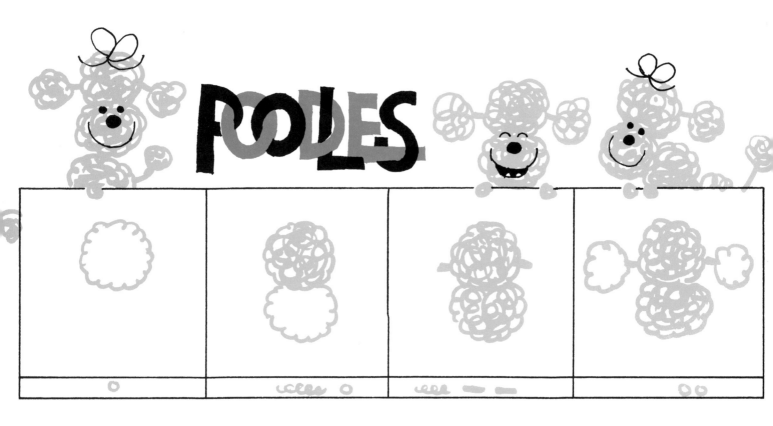

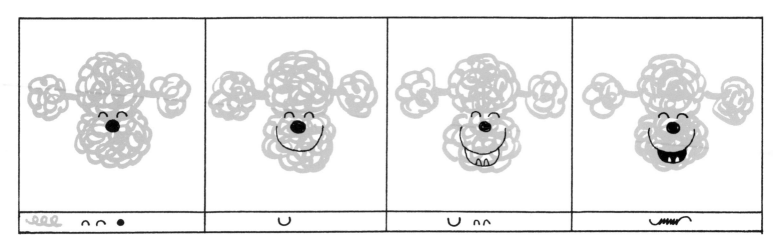

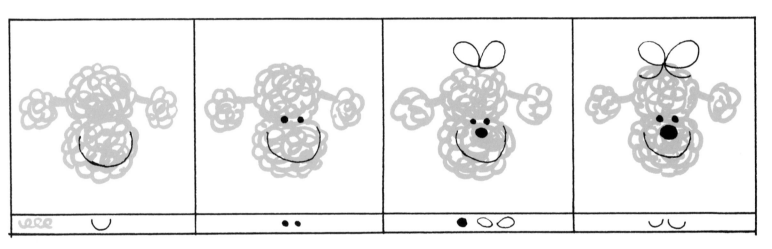

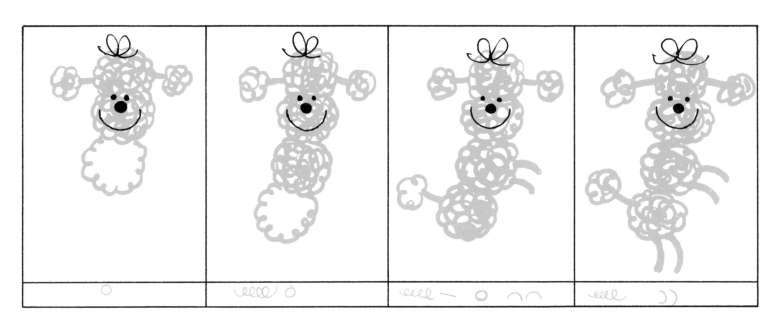

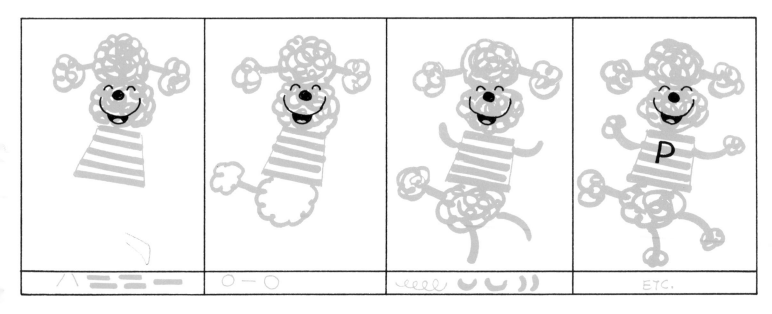

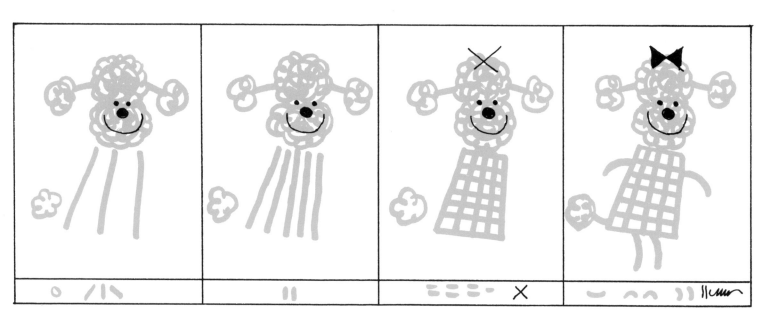

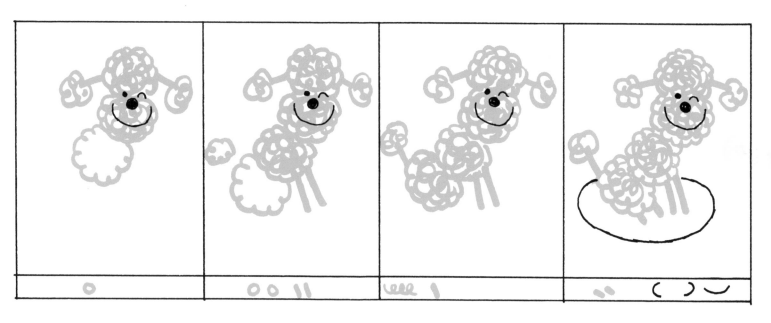

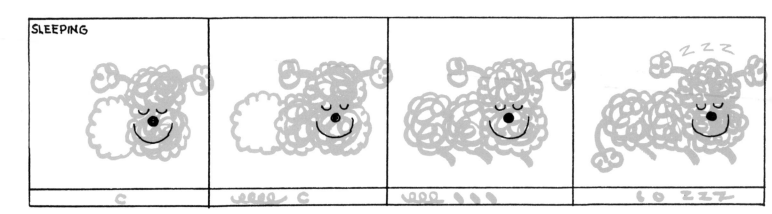

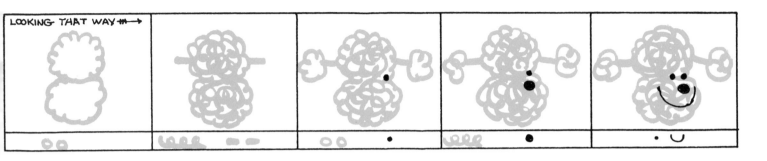

LOOKING THAT WAY ‖→

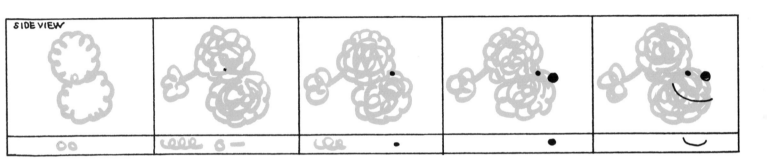

SIDE VIEW

SOME OTHER WAYS
TO MAKE POODLES

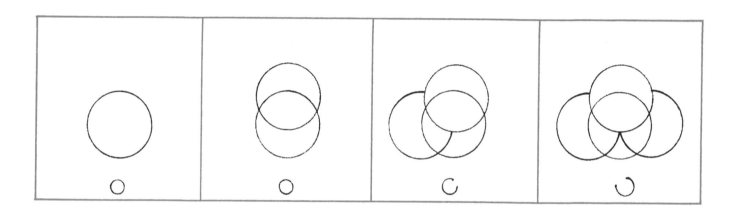

THESE ANIMALS WERE MADE BY DRAWING AROUND A PENNY.
IF YOU WANT TO MAKE A LARGER ANIMAL YOU CAN DRAW
AROUND A CAN OR PLATE OR EVEN USE A COMPASS !!!

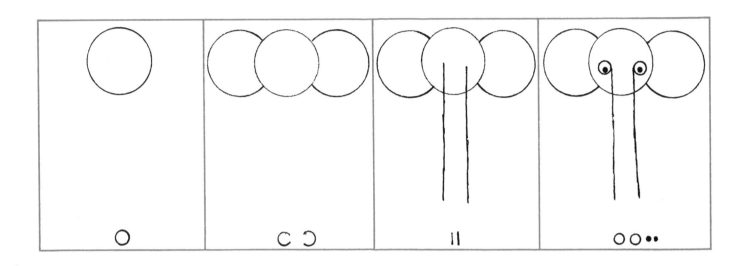

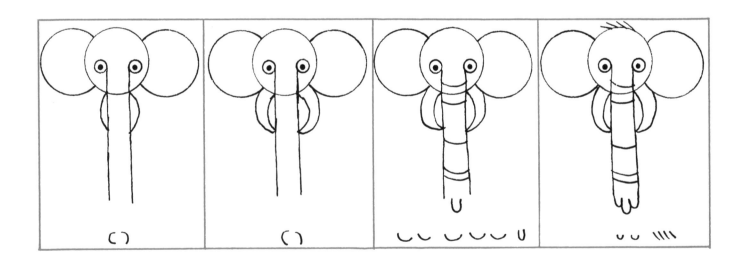

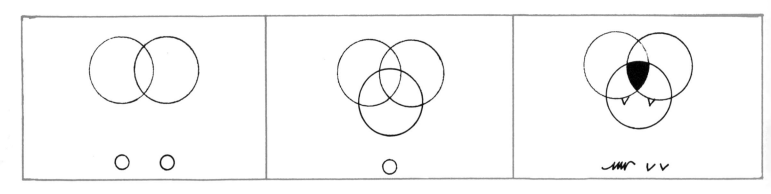

THINGS PIRATICAL

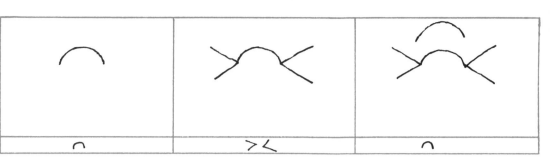

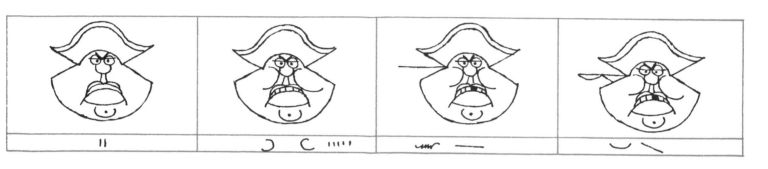

FLEABANE

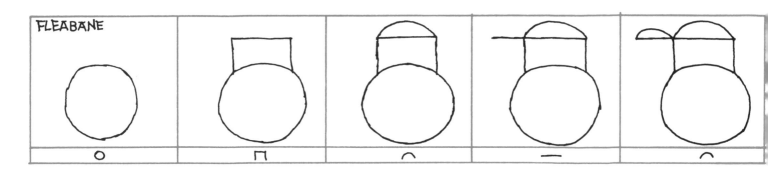

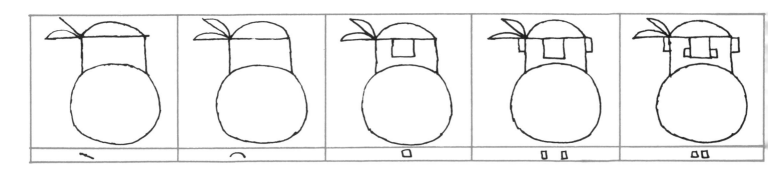

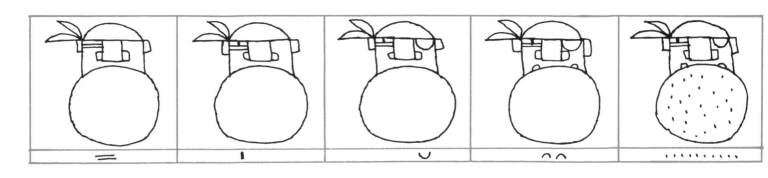

TWIST

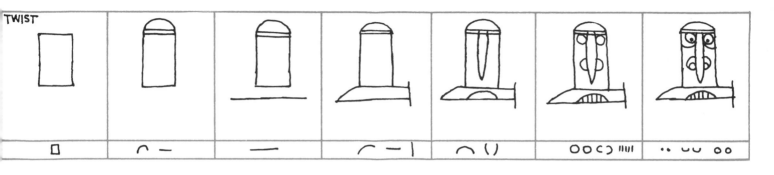

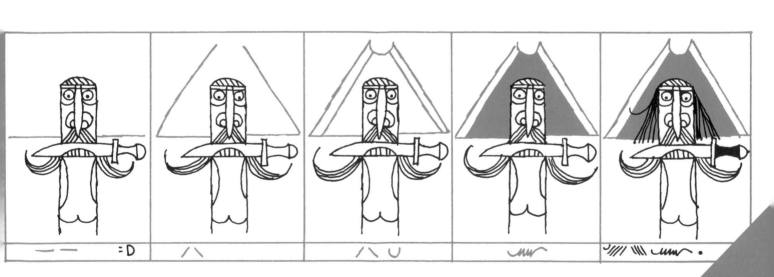

MORE
TWIST

CHEST

RIGHT ARM

FOR HAND ⇶→
SEE PAGE 38.

LEGS

BOOTS ETC.

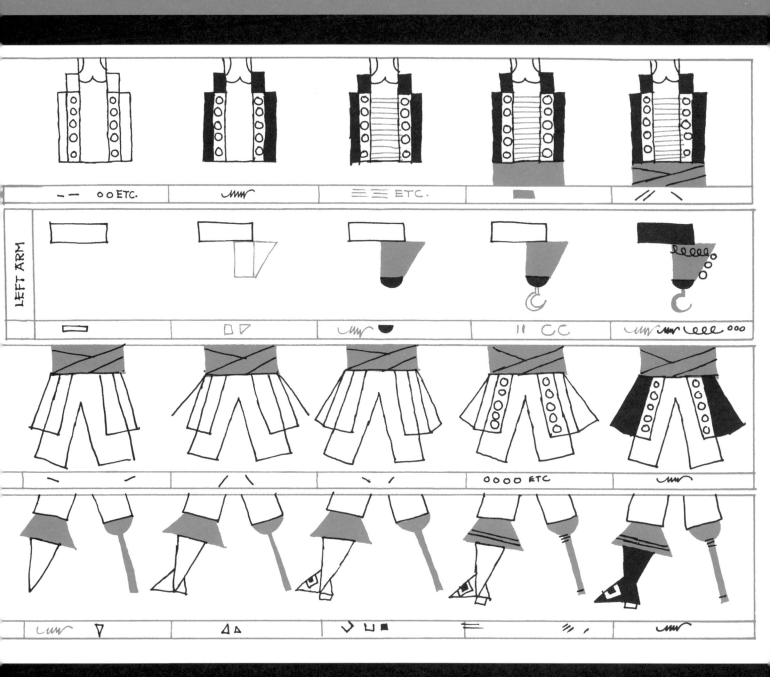

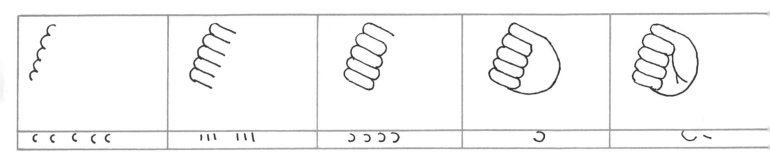

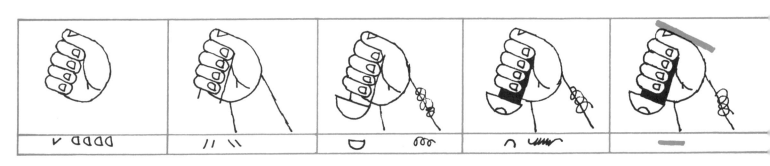

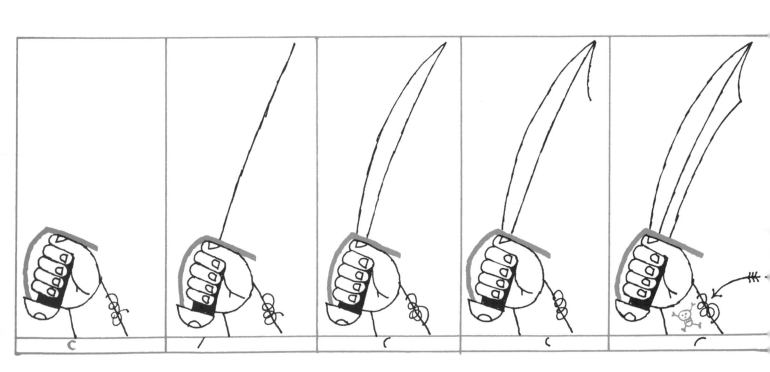

THOSE FINGERS

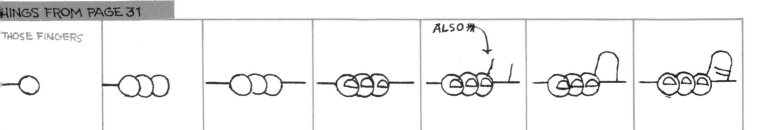

ALSO

—○   ↺↺   —   ◠◠◠ || ∩   =

THAT ROPE

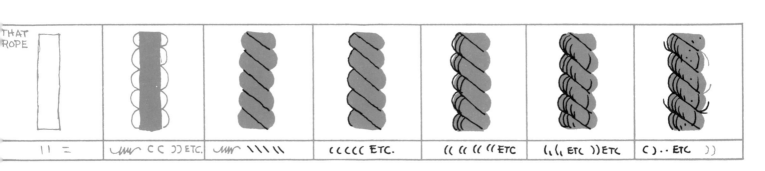

|| =   ᴗᴗᴗ CC JJ ETC.   ᴗᴗᴗ \\\\ || ((((ETC.   ((((((((ETC   (, (, ETC)) ETC   C) .. ETC))

THAT HOOK

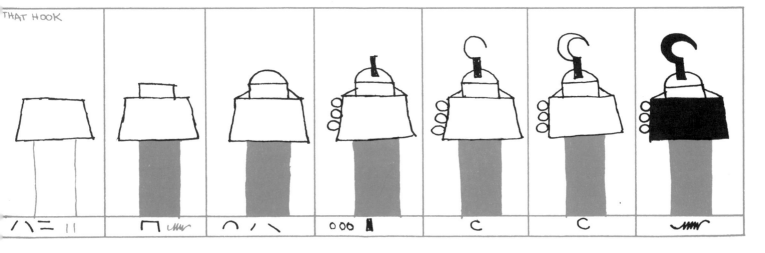

∧∧ = || ⊓ ᴗᴗᴗ   ∩ ∕∕   ०॰॰ | C   C   ᴗᴗᴗ

TATTOO

○   ⊔   ᴗ | || • • •   \\ //   •• •• •• ••

PIRATE'S PISTOL

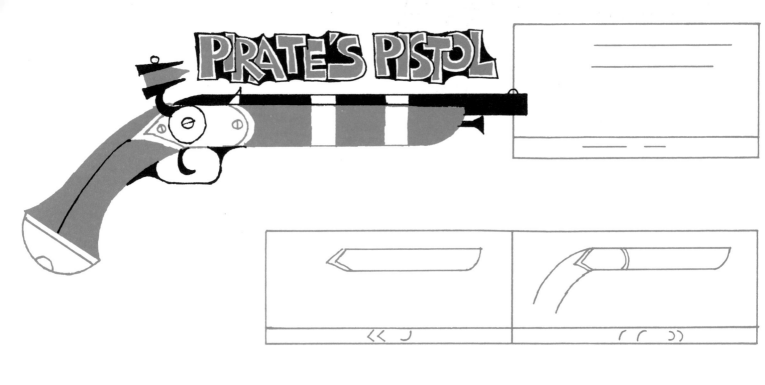

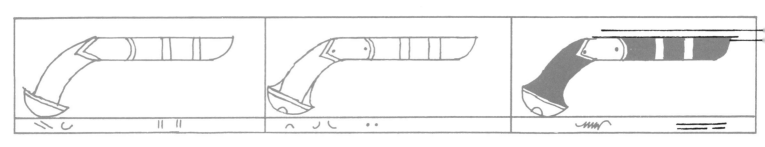

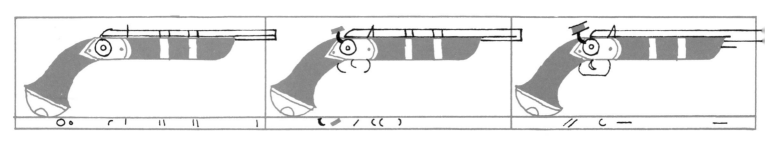

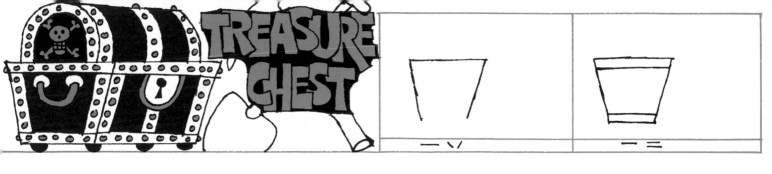

TREASURE CHEST

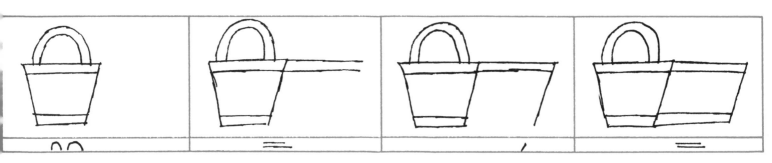

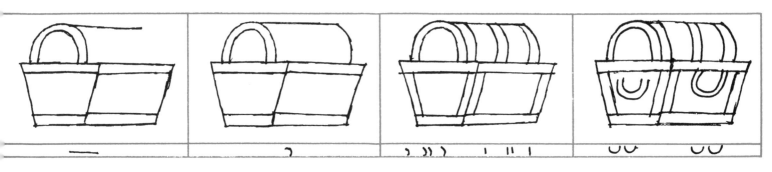

ALSO

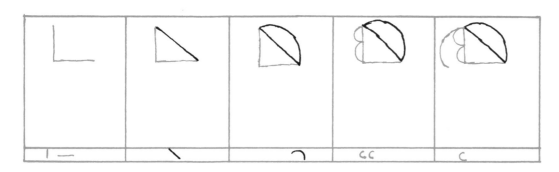

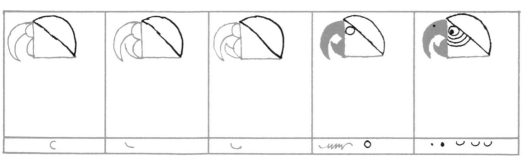

PIRATE PARROT

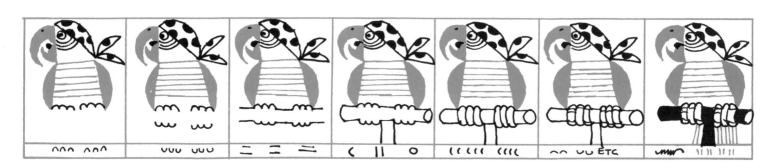

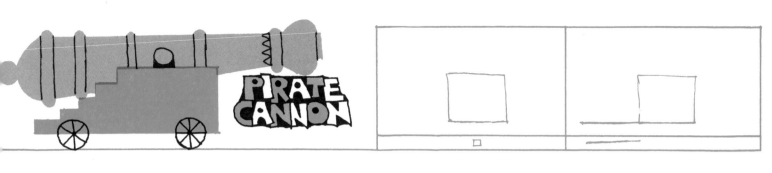

PIRATE CANNON

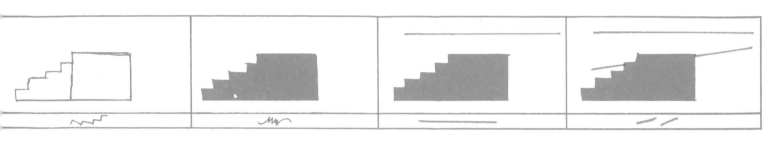

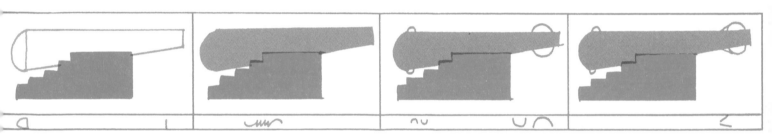

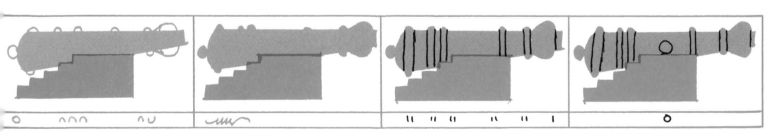

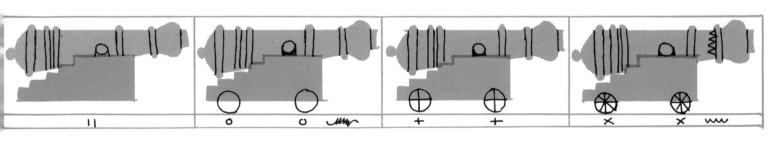

Sea Hawk

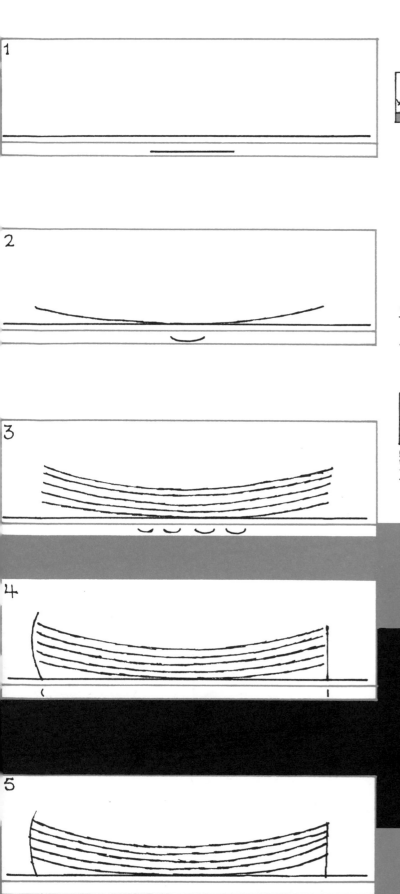

1

2

3

4

5

I FIND IT EASIER TO DRAW BACK AND FORTH LINES ←→ THAN UP AND DOWN LINES...↕ SO, WHEN I HAVE TO DRAW LONG, STRAIGHT, UP AND DOWN LINES I OFTEN TURN MY PAPER AROUND LIKE THIS.

IF MY LINES ARE STILL NOT AS STRAIGHT AS I WOULD LIKE I USE A STRAIGHT EDGE SUCH AS A RULER OR A PIECE OF CARDBOARD.

TILTED MASTS

AN OLD PAD BACK MAKES A GOOD STRAIGHT EDGE.

TRIANGLE
"T" SQUARE

IF I AM WORRIED ABOUT MY MASTS BEING TILTED (SOMETIMES I DO, SOMETIMES I DO NOT) I WILL USE A "T" SQUARE AND A TRIANGLE...IF I DO NOT HAVE THESE TOOLS I USE THE CORNER OF AN OLD PAD BACK, LIKE THIS.⤸

DECIDE WHERE YOU WANT TO PUT YOUR MASTS.

LINE ONE EDGE OF PAD BACK UP WITH WATERLINE.

DRAW ALONG THE OTHER EDGE.

VOILA !!!

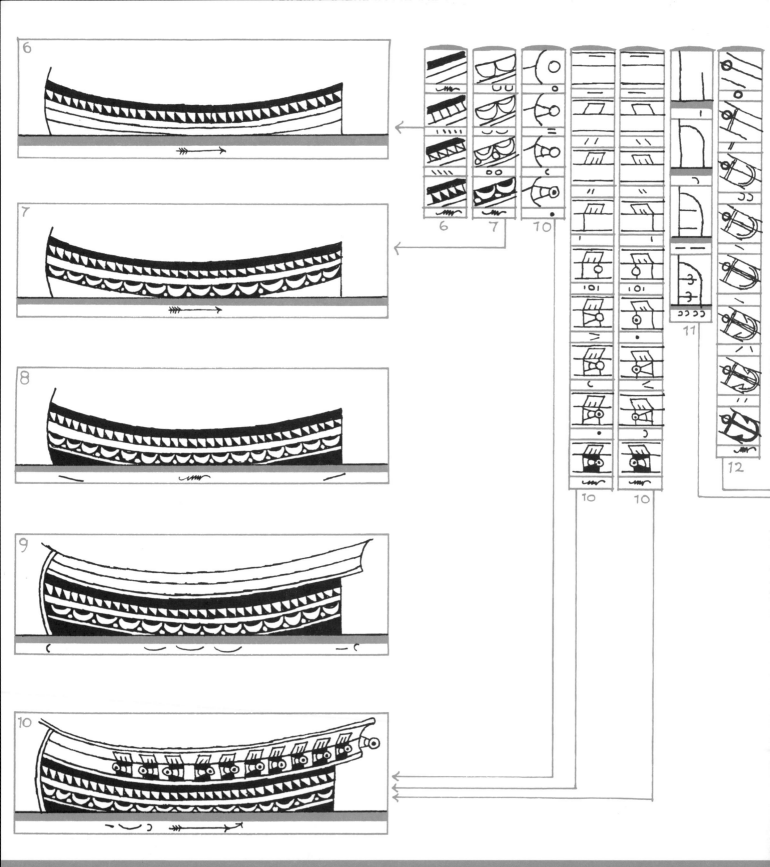

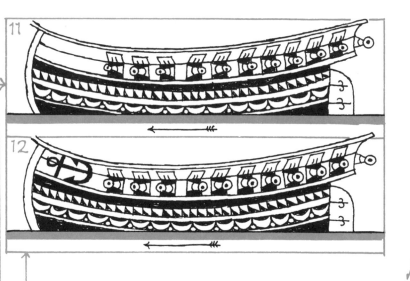

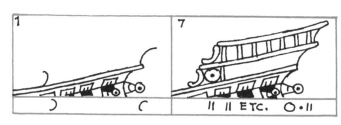

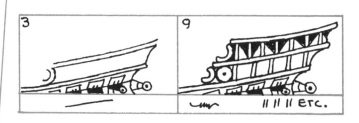

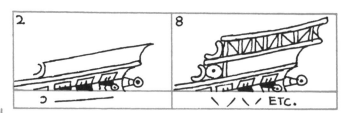

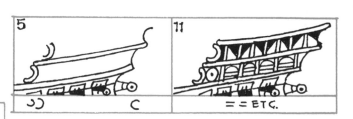

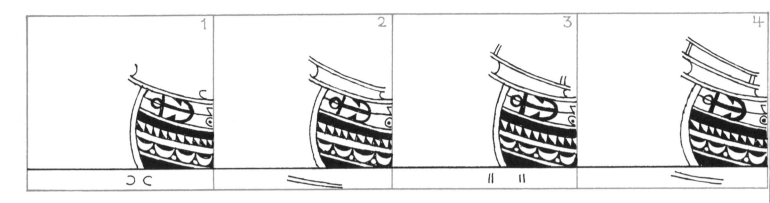

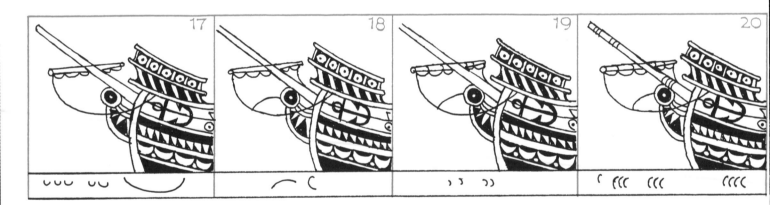

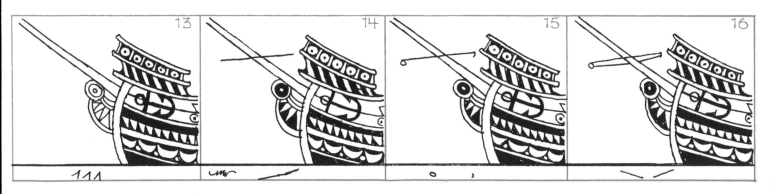

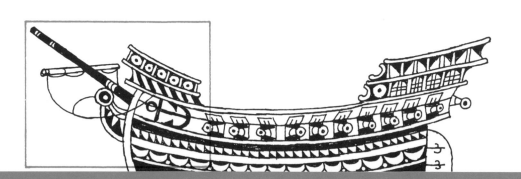

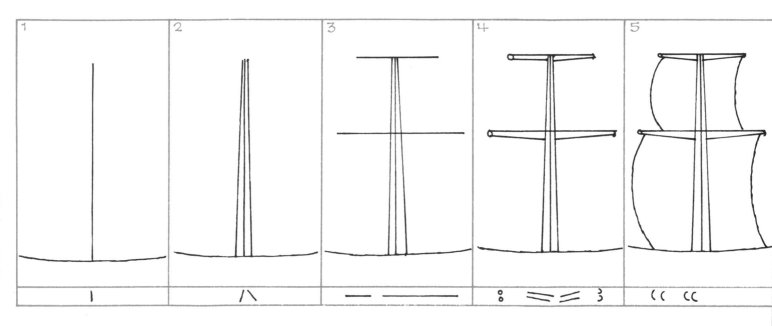

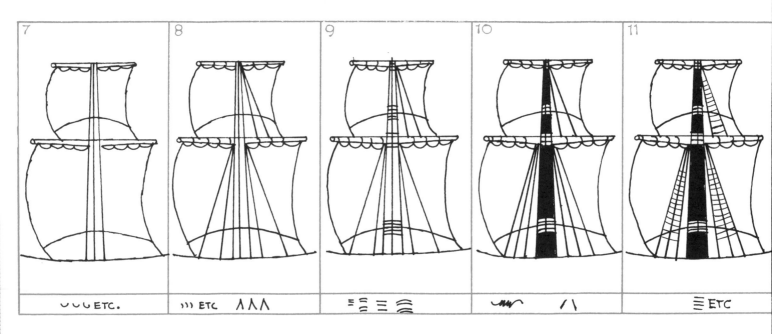

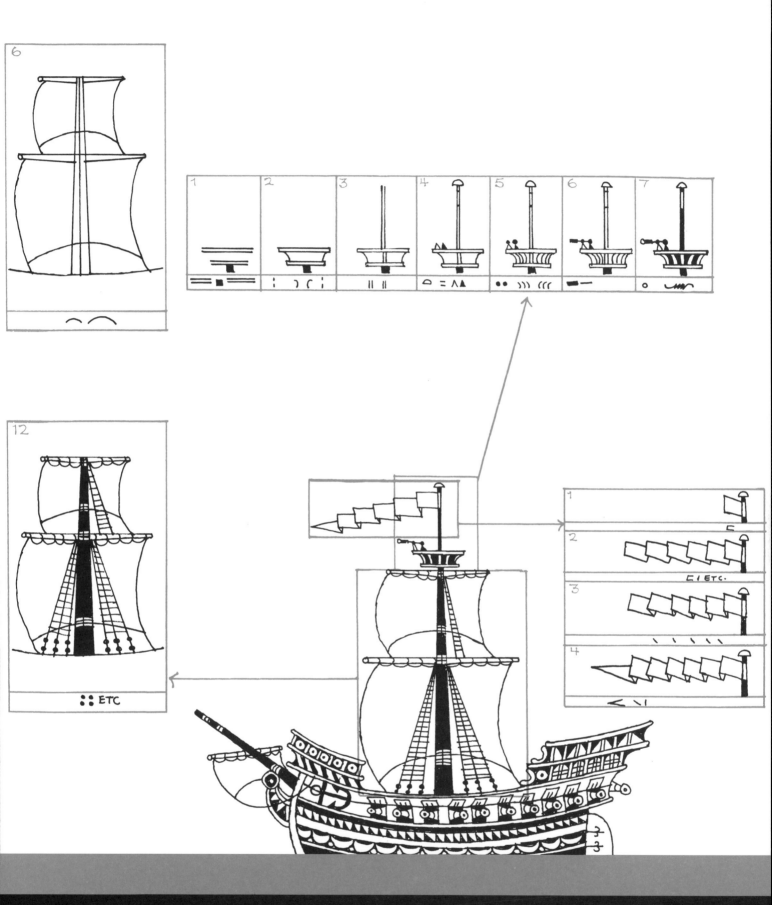

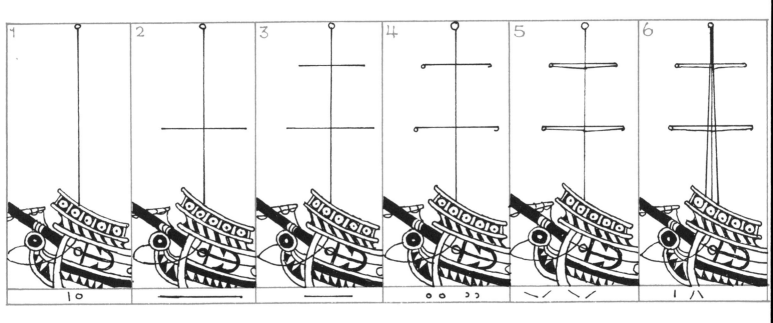

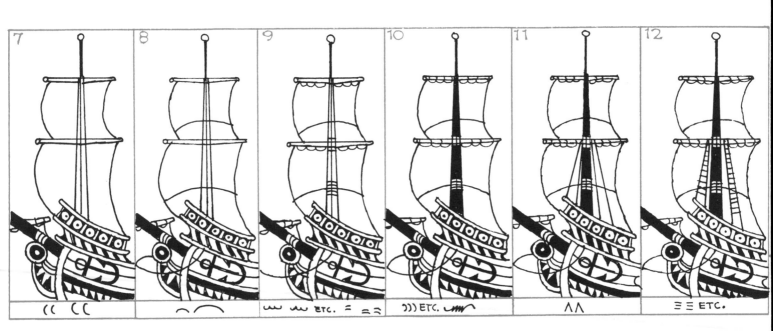

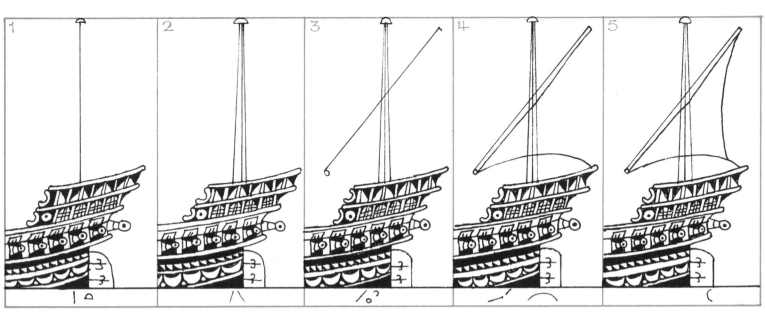

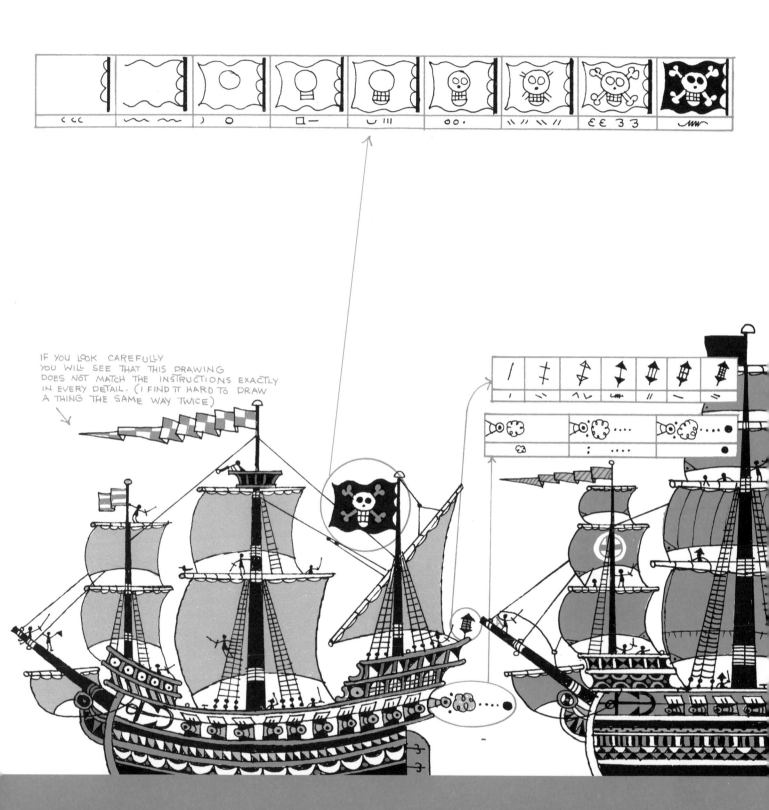

IF YOU LOOK CAREFULLY
YOU WILL SEE THAT THIS DRAWING
DOES NOT MATCH THE INSTRUCTIONS EXACTLY
IN EVERY DETAIL. (I FIND IT HARD TO DRAW
A THING THE SAME WAY TWICE)

THERE ARE MANY WAYS YOU CAN CHANGE THE "SEA HAWK" TO "BUILD" A DIFFERENT
SHIP. FOR INSTANCE, YOU CAN ADD MORE MASTS, SAILS OR ROWS OF CANNON.
YOU CAN CHANGE THE DECORATIONS AND/OR COLOR. YOU CAN USE
STRAIGHT LINES FOR THE HULL. USING THIS BASIC IDEA YOU CAN
MAKE YOUR OWN NAVY, FLEET OR ARMADA !

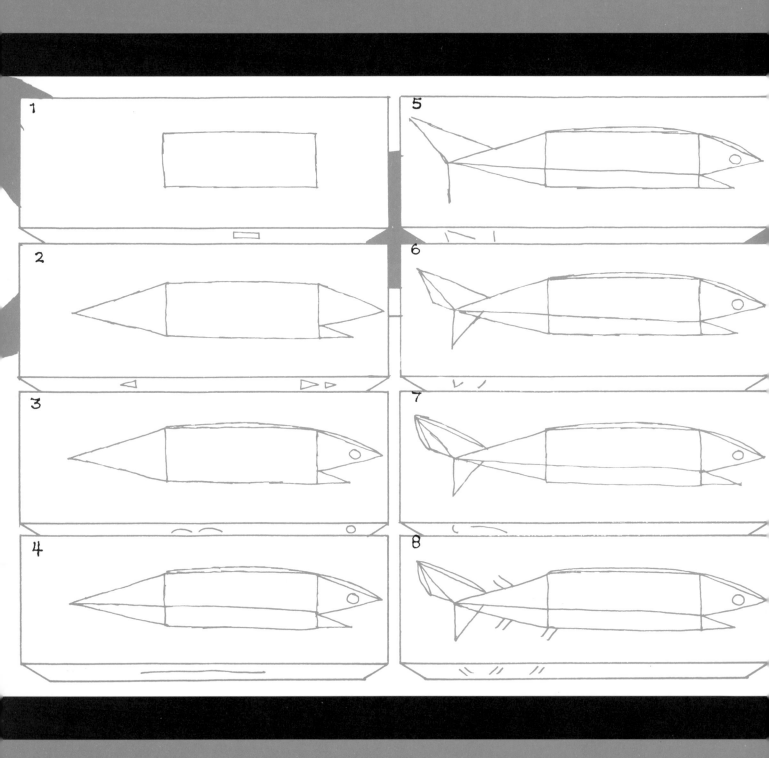

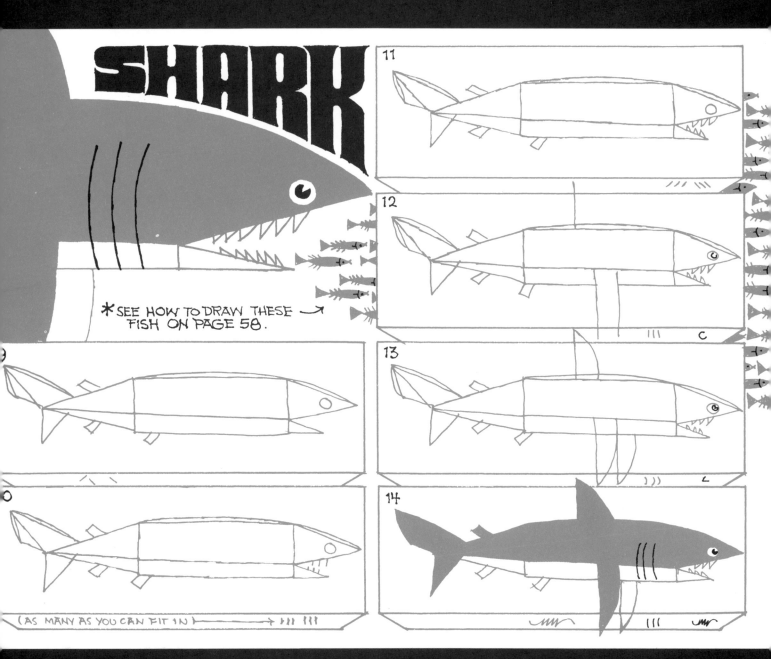

SHARK

*SEE HOW TO DRAW THESE FISH ON PAGE 58.

(AS MANY AS YOU CAN FIT IN) →

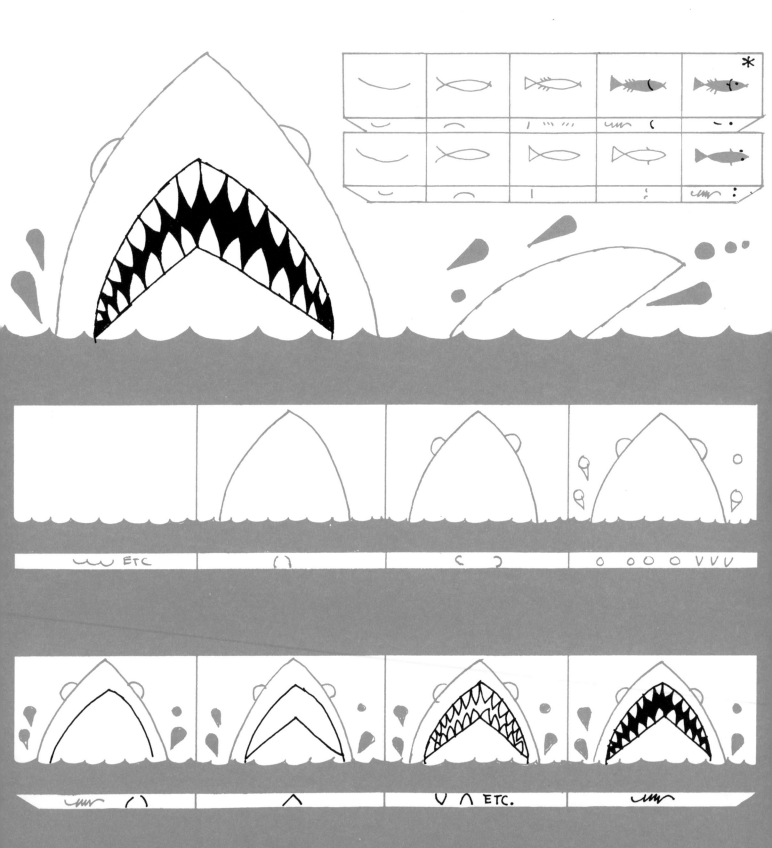

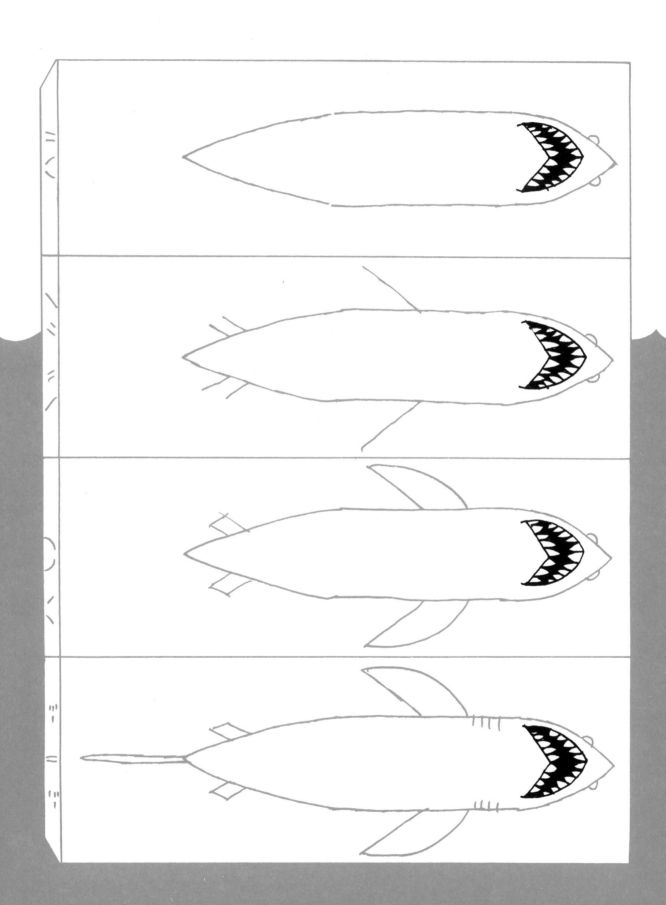

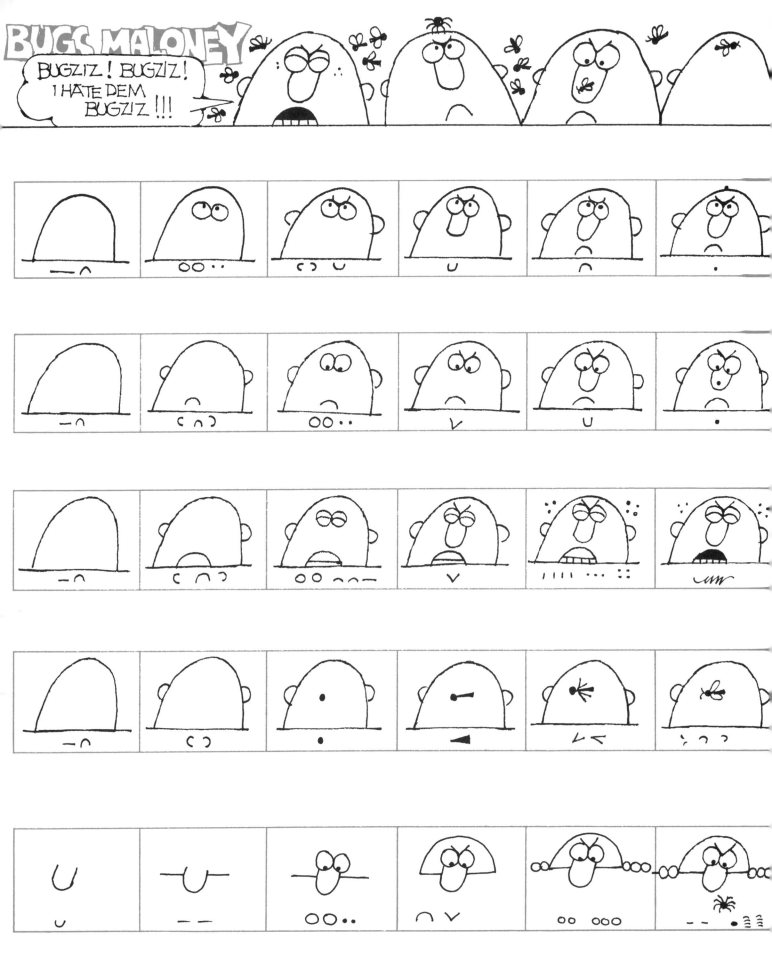

DEM BUGZIZ

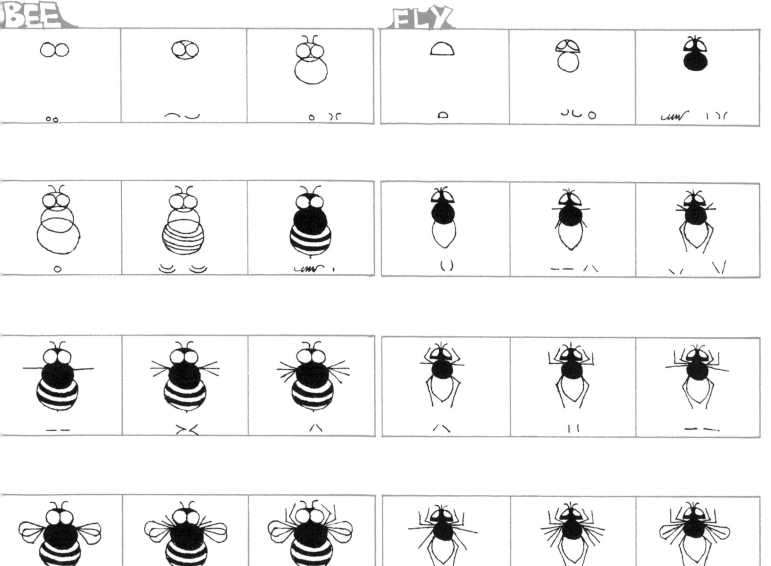

ANT

CRICKET

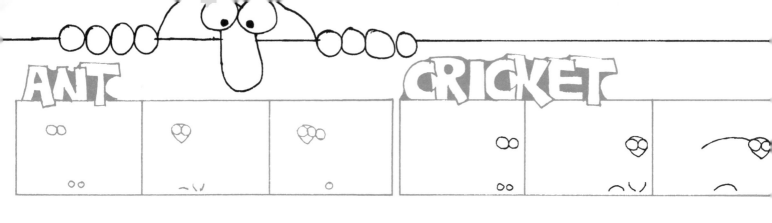

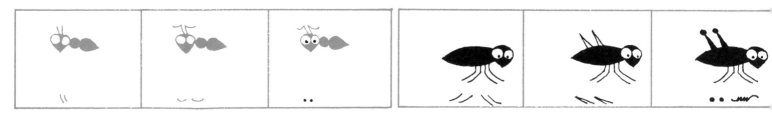

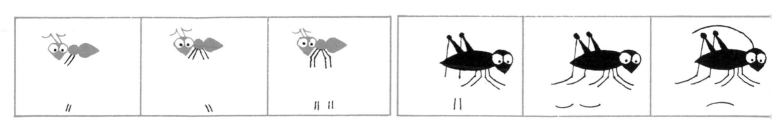

SPIDER

GRASSHOPPER

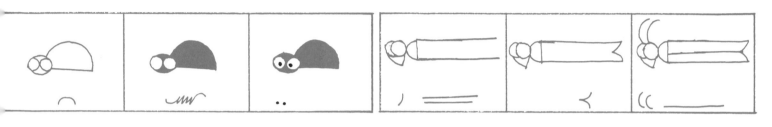

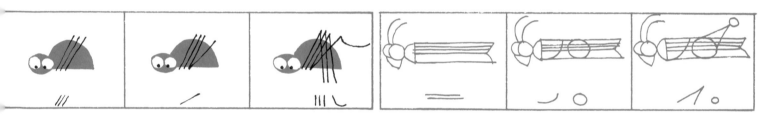

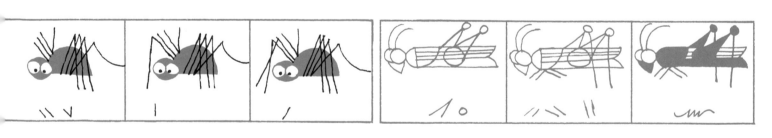

ALSO

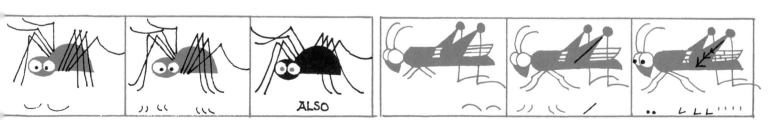

SKEETER   # CENTIPEDE

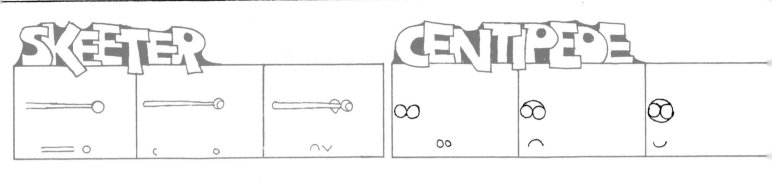

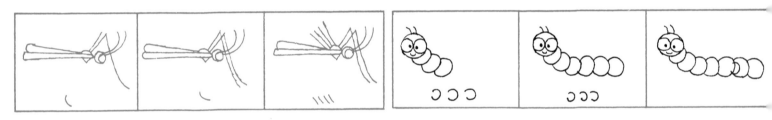

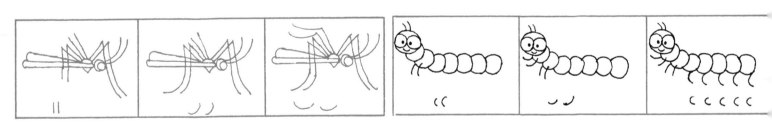

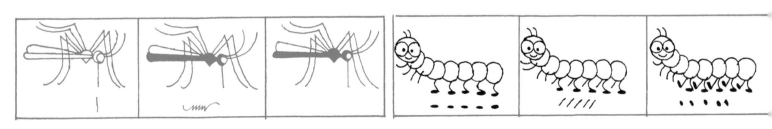

PRAVING MANTIS

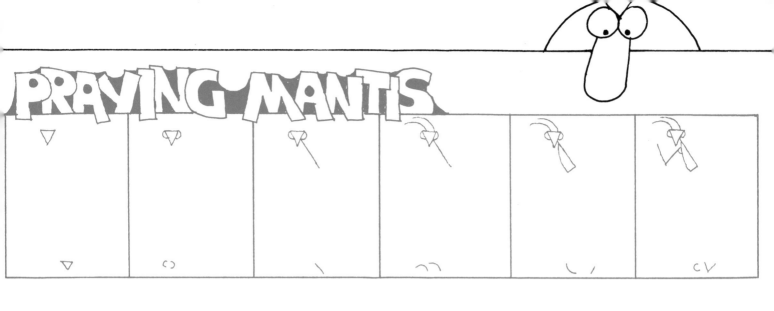

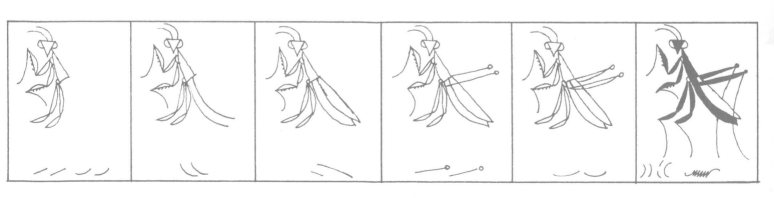

SWAMP CREATURE

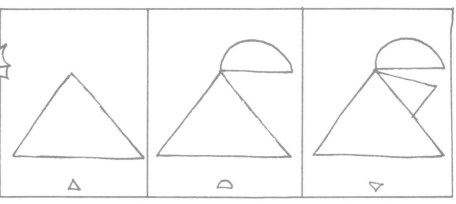

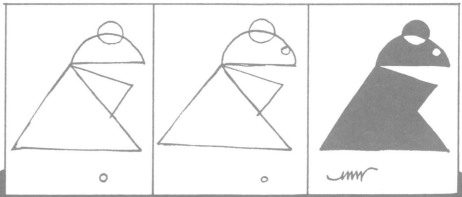

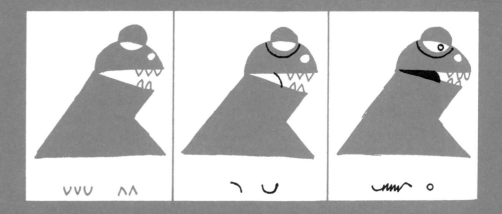

* "DRACULA" IS IN THE BIG GREEN DRAWING BOOK.   MORE CREATURES IN THE BIG ORANGE DRAWING BOOK.

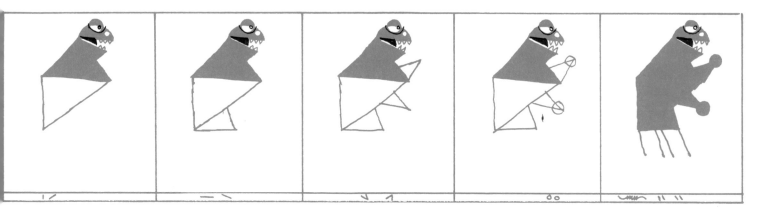

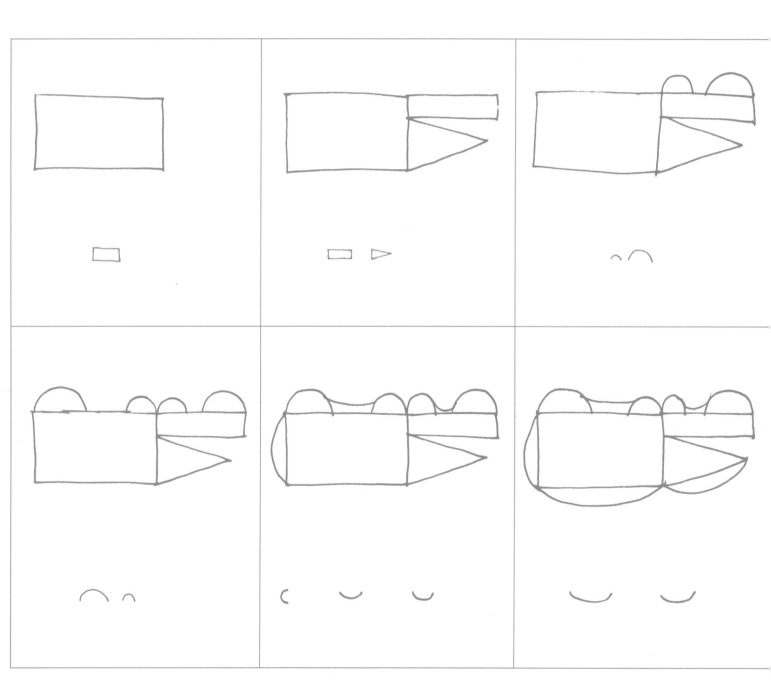

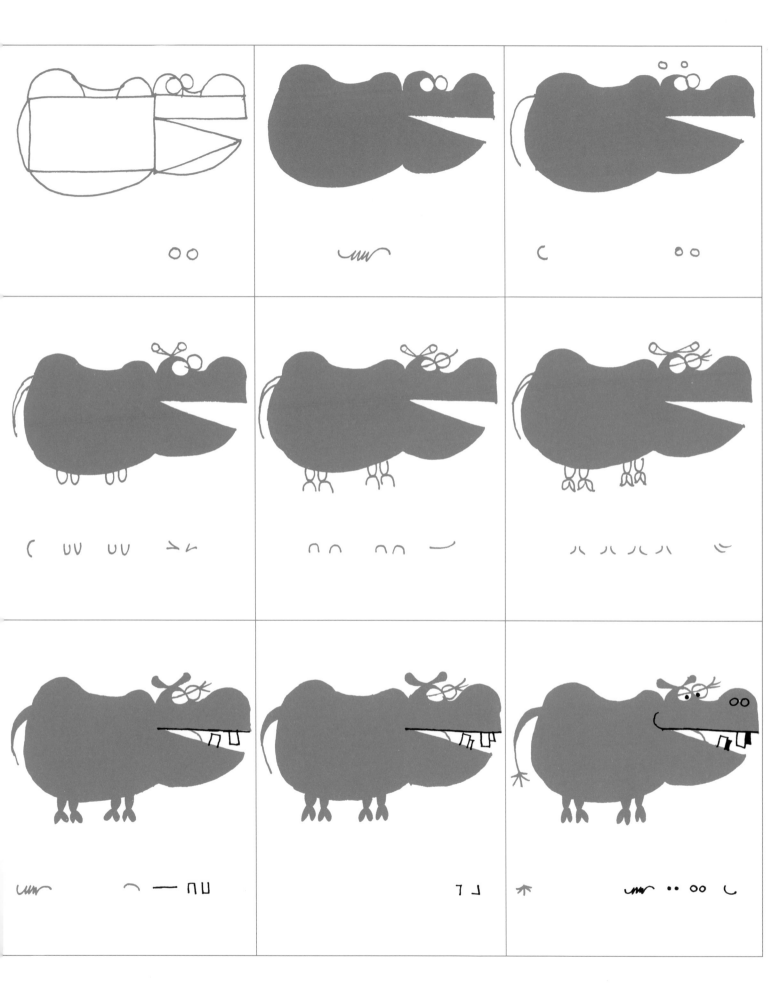

OTHER LESS GRAND BUT VERY NICE HIPPOS

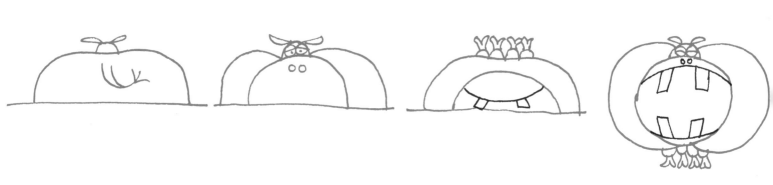

SWIMMING   SWIMMING   DEAD HIPPO   YAWNING

ALSO   ALSO

71

THE GUPPY

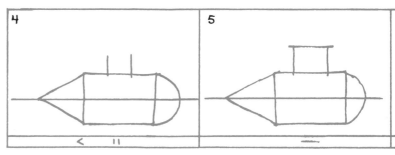

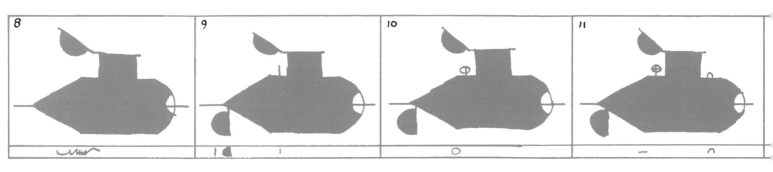

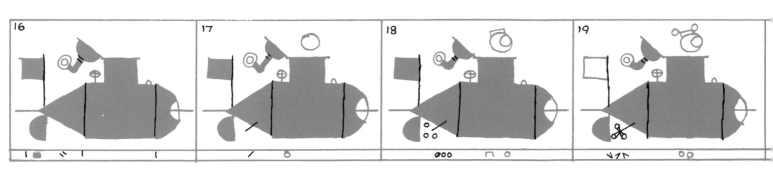

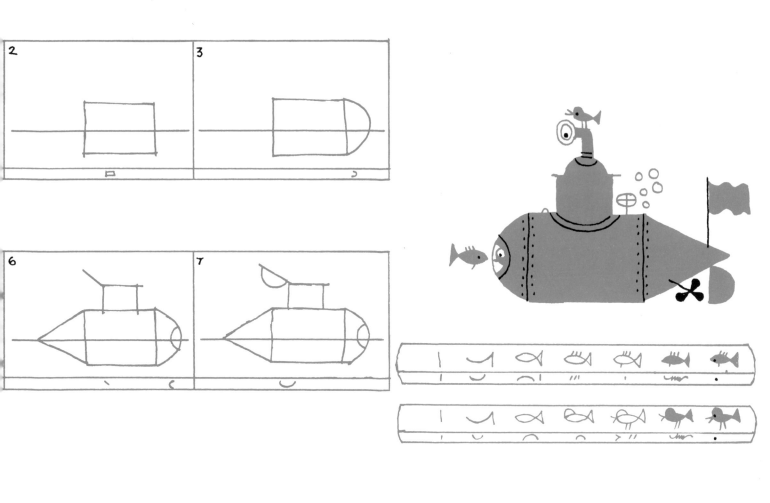

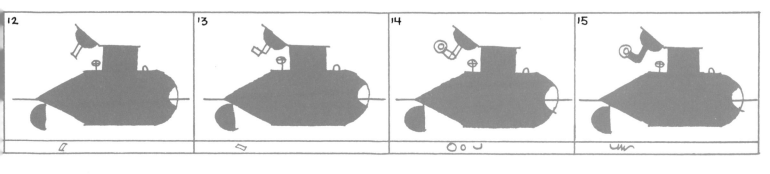

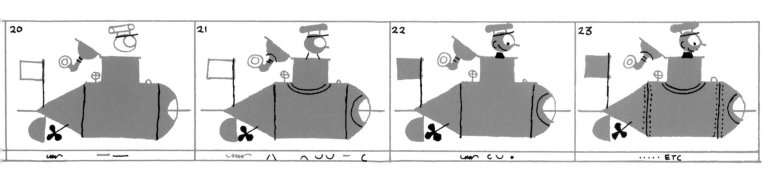

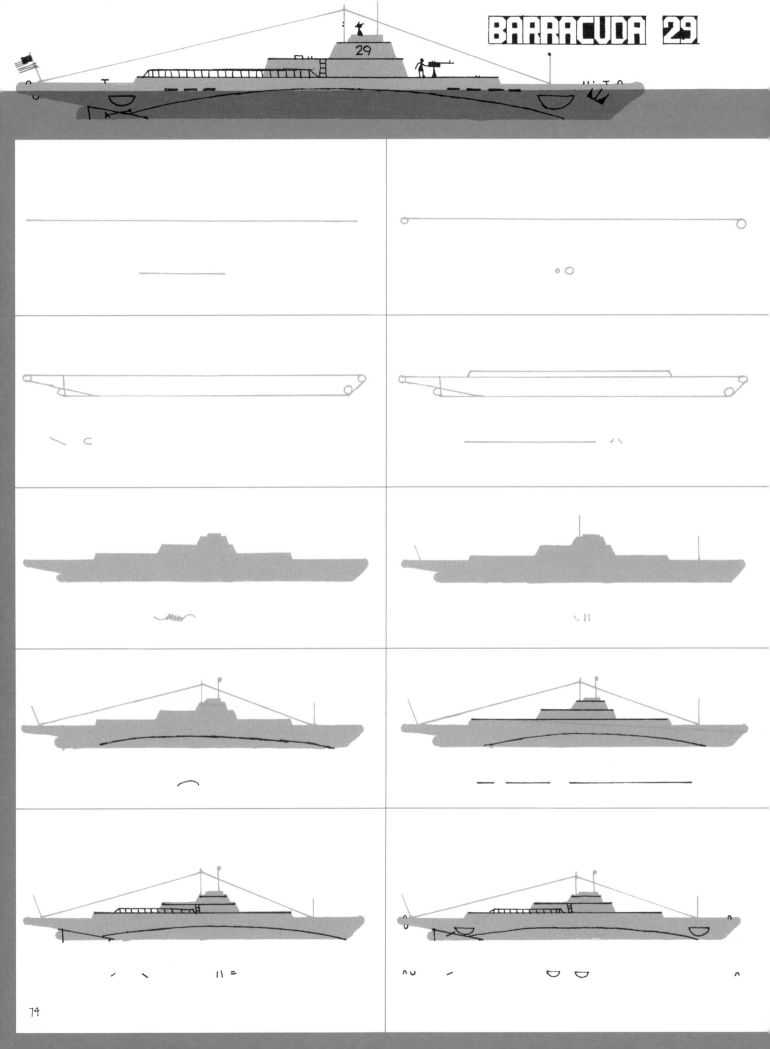

BARRACUDA 29

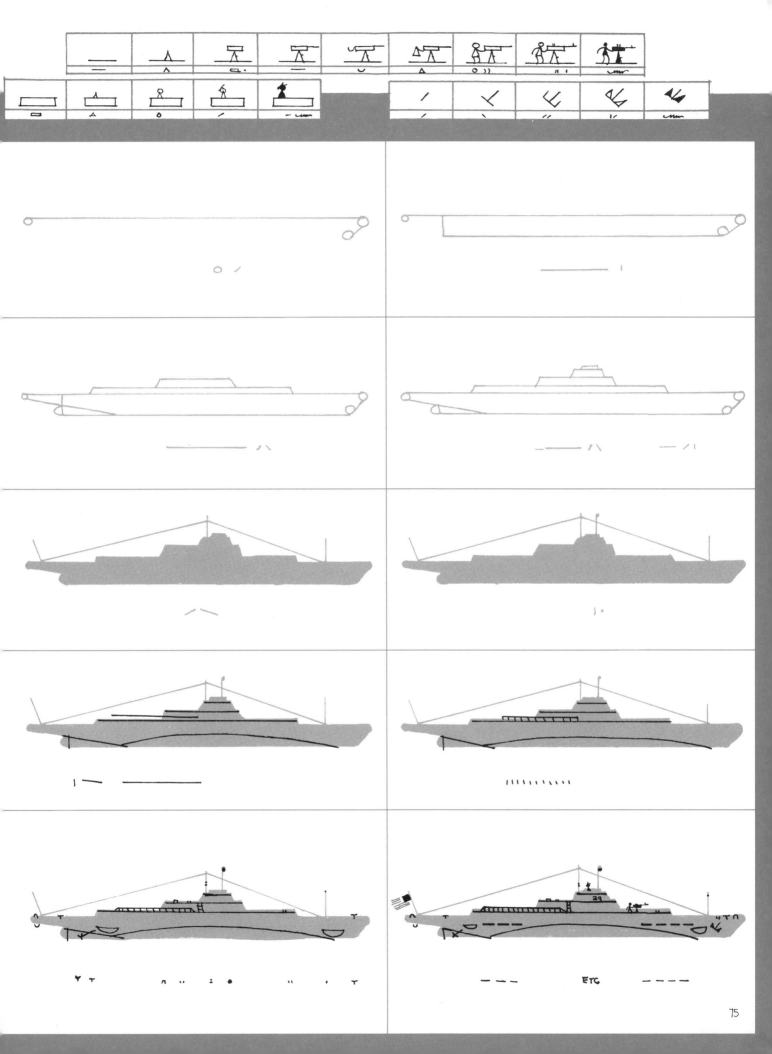

40 YEARS AGO SOMEONE SHOWED ME HOW
TO DRAW THESE 3 THINGS.
I STILL REMEMBER HOW TO DRAW THEM.
DRAWING THEM TURNED A LITTLE LIGHT ON
IN MY MIND, GAVE ME MANY HOURS OF PLEASURE
AND BECAME THE INSPIRATION FOR A SERIES
OF DRAWING BOOKS OF WHICH THIS IS ONE.
I FIGURED IT WAS ABOUT TIME THAT I
PASSED THEM ON. PERHAPS ONE DAY
SOME OF YOU WILL IN TURN PASS THEM ON
TO SOMEONE ELSE.

Ed Emberley

IPSWICH, MASS. JAN. 1981

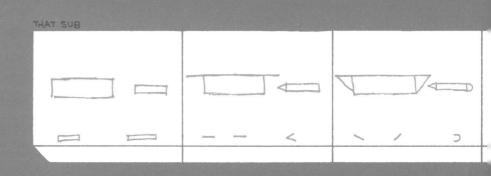

THAT SHIP

THAT SUB

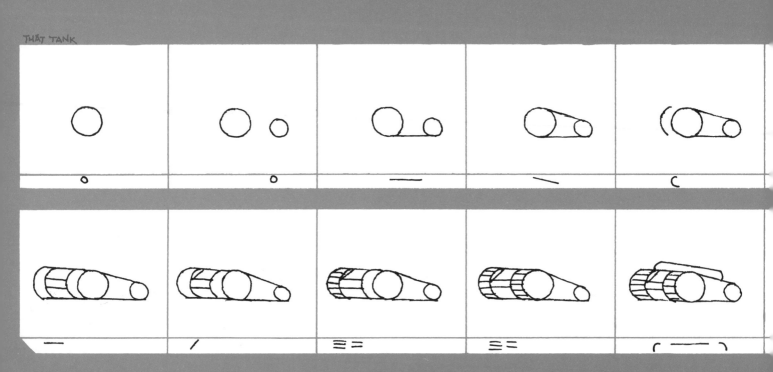

THAT TANK

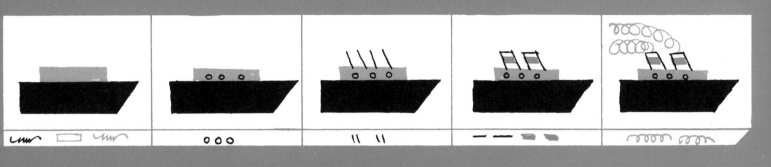

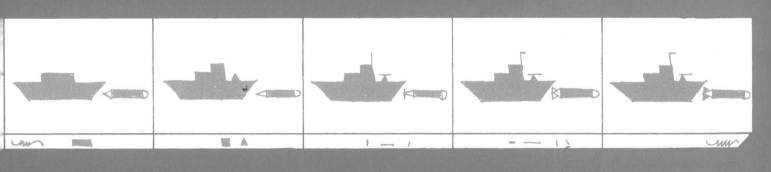

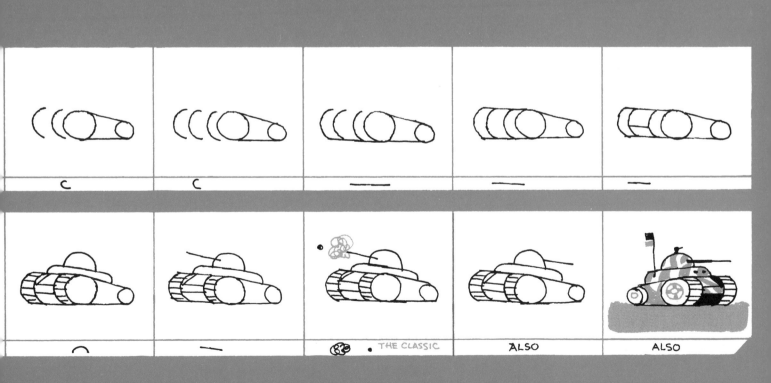

THE CLASSIC

ALSO

ALSO

BASIC TRUCK

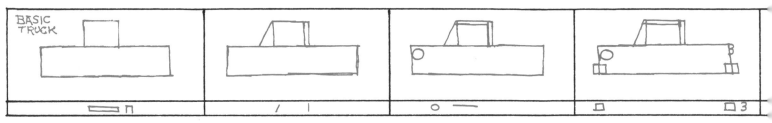

FISH TRUCK

WITH COVER

BUILDER'S TRUCK

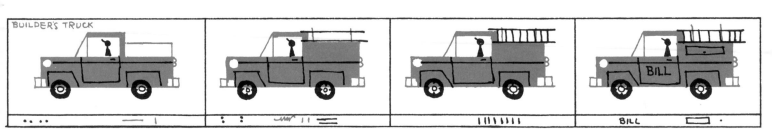

VAN

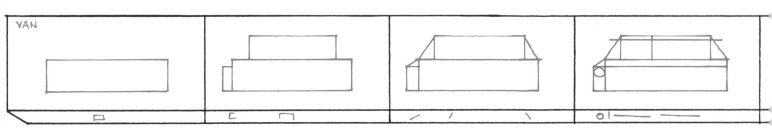

TOW TRUCK

TIRES
LOWER!

* NOTE LARGER TIRES AND BUMPERS

TOW

CAMPER

HAY

ETC.

PLOW

ETC.

ETC.

PARK

ETC.

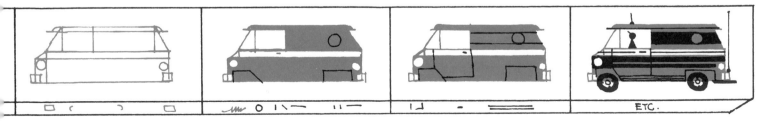

ETC.

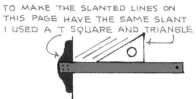

TO MAKE THE SLANTED LINES ON THIS PAGE HAVE THE SAME SLANT I USED A T SQUARE AND TRIANGLE

BUT MOST OF THE TIME I JUST GUESS AND DRAW THEM FREE HAND.

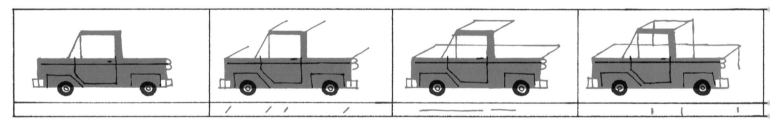

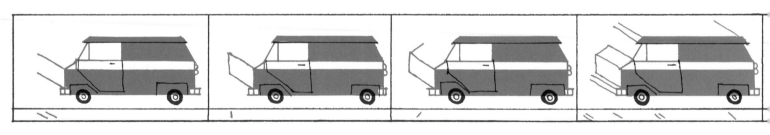

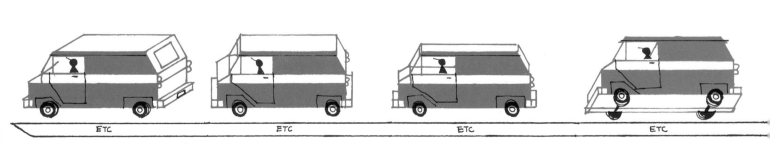

ETC   ETC   ETC   ETC

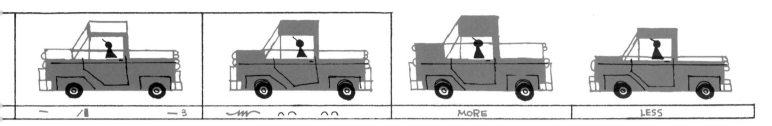

- — /| — 3 | ~ 00 00 | MORE | LESS

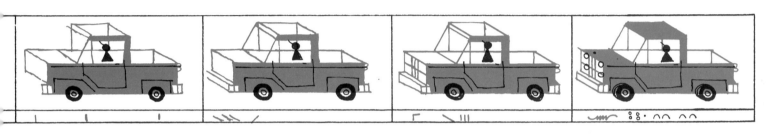

| | | | ///// / | ⌐)/// | ~ °°·°° 00 00

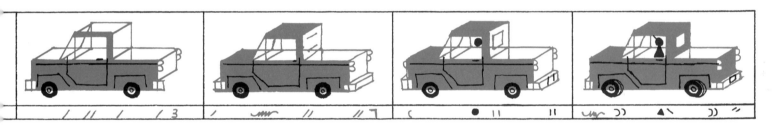

/ // / / 3 | / ~ // //7 | ⊂ • || || | ~)) ▲\ )) ~

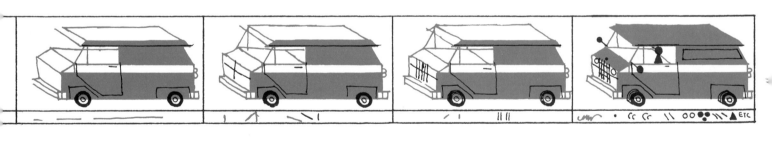

— — — | / ↑ \ \| | / / || || | ~ · ((((|| 00 ●● ||| ▲ ETC

FOR THOSE OF YOU WHO WILL
BE USING A T SQUARE AND
TRIANGLE THIS INFORMATION
MIGHT BE USEFUL.

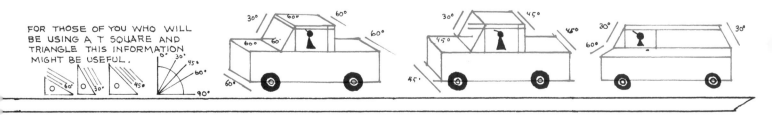

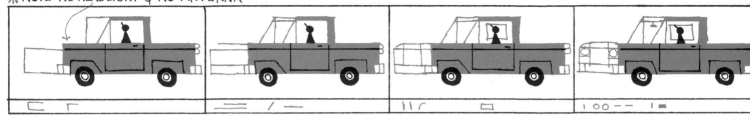

※ NOTE NO HEADLIGHT & NO ANTENNA

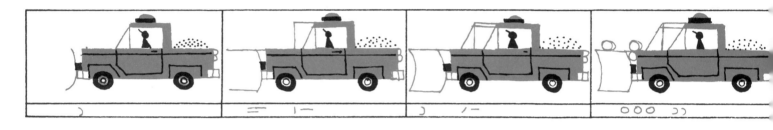

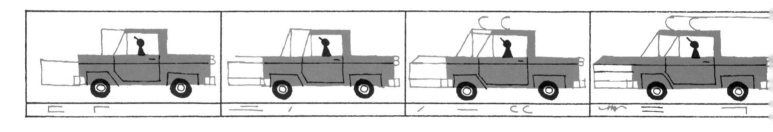

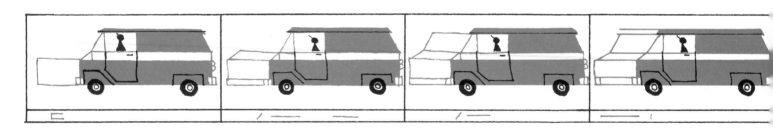

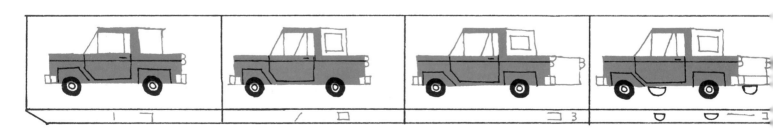

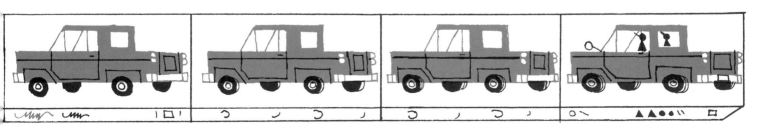

A NEEBORT
FROO

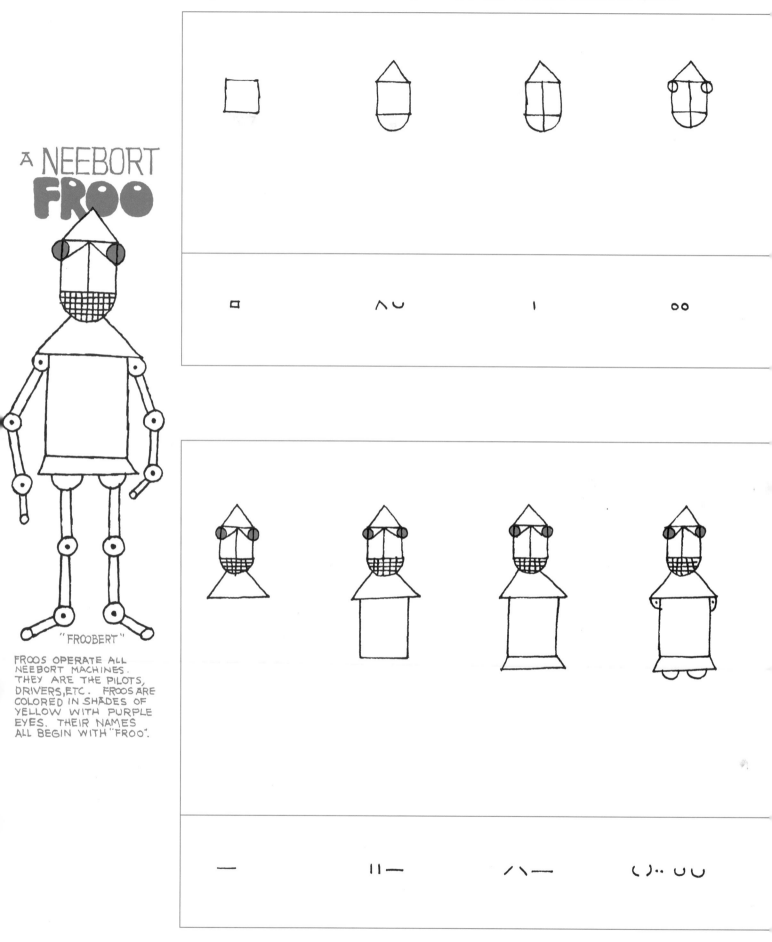

"FROOBERT"

FROOS OPERATE ALL
NEEBORT MACHINES.
THEY ARE THE PILOTS,
DRIVERS, ETC. FROOS ARE
COLORED IN SHADES OF
YELLOW WITH PURPLE
EYES. THEIR NAMES
ALL BEGIN WITH "FROO".

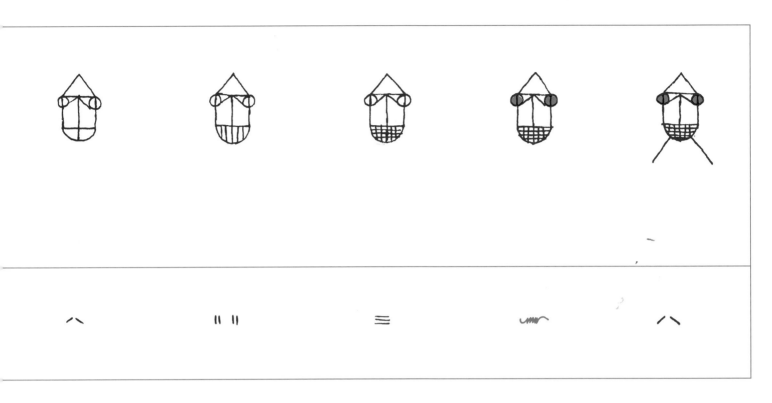

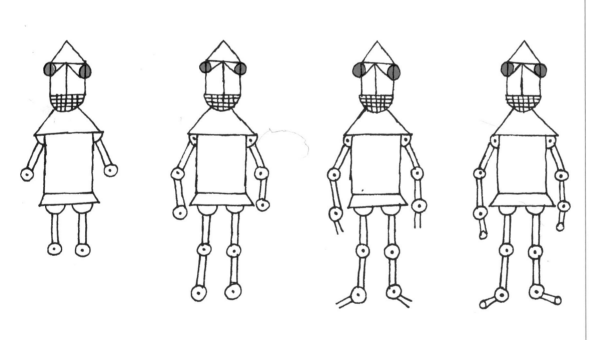

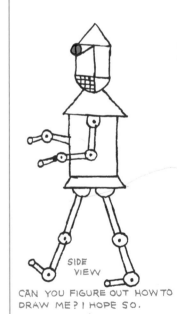

SIDE
VIEW
CAN YOU FIGURE OUT HOW TO
DRAW ME? I HOPE SO.

//O· \\O· 110·110· ||o· ||o· ||o· ||o· || || // || oo   oo

A FROOTER

THE MOST COMMON NEEBORT VEHICLE IS A FROO SCOOTER (CALLED A FROOTER) IT IS A 3 WHEELED ALL PURPOSE VEHICLE USE FOR PICK UP AND DELIVERY. IT HAS A NUMBER OF TRAILERS AND OTHER USEFUL ATTACHMENTS.
* FROOS HAVE THEIR OWN LIGHT FOR SEEING IN THE DARK. THIS LIGHT IS CALLED FROOSEE.

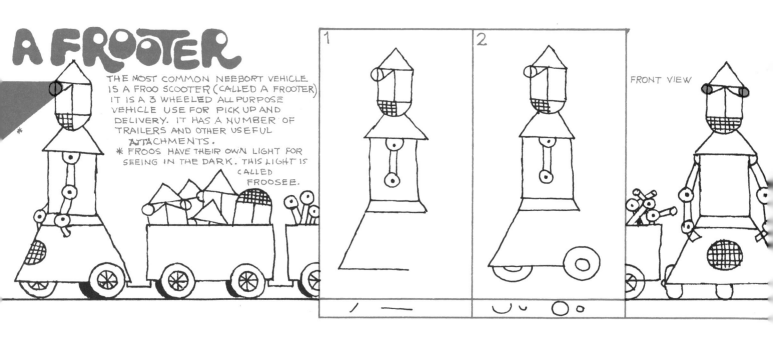

FRONT VIEW

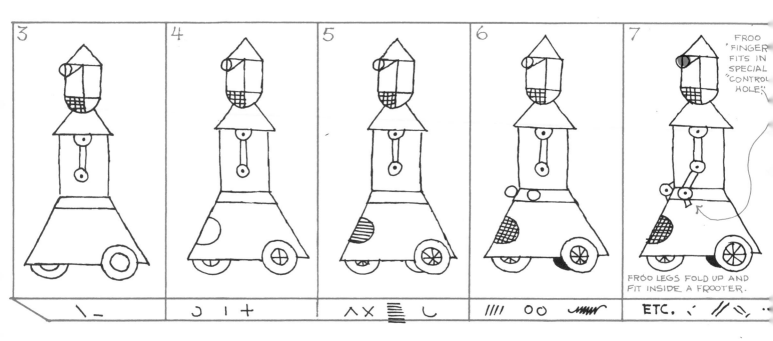

FROO FINGER FITS IN SPECIAL "CONTROL HOLE"

FROO LEGS FOLD UP AND FIT INSIDE A FROOTER.

ETC.

A NEEBORT TRAKIR

THESE HEAVY DUTY
BASIC UNITS ARE USED ALONE AND
ARE USED AS PARTS OF LARGER MACHINES
USED FOR EXPLORATION, MINING,
DEFENSE AND OTHER SIMILAR TASKS
SUCH AS EARTH MOVING. (CALLED ZORT
MOVING ON THE PLANET ZORT* AND
FRED MOVING ON FRED **)

* SEE PAGE 82 BIG GREEN DRAWING BOOK.
** SEE PAGE 91 THIS BOOK

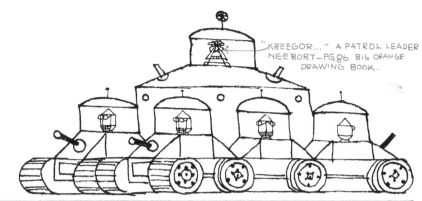

"KREEGOR..." A PATROL LEADER
NEEBORT—PG 86 BIG ORANGE
DRAWING BOOK.

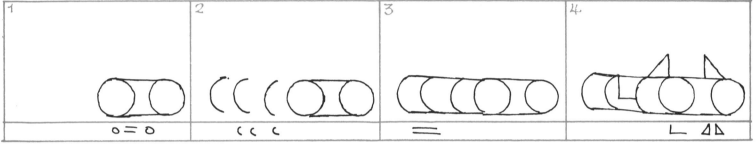

1

2

o = o

c c c

3

=

4

L △△

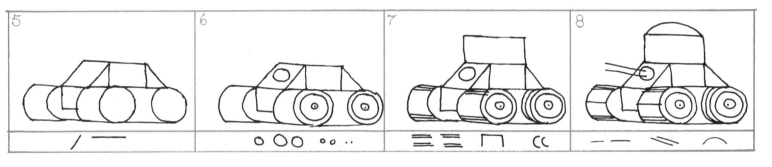

5

/ —

6

o o O O o o ..

7

= = = = ⊓ C C

8

- - — \ \ ⌒

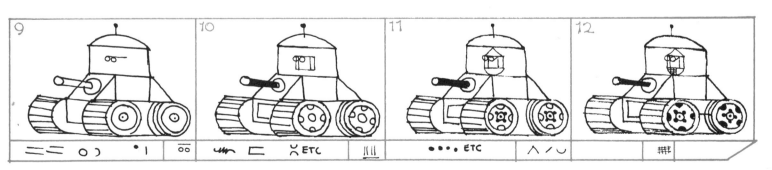

9

= = ⌒ o) • l   oo

10

⌒ ⌐ ⋎ ETC ||||

11

• • • • ETC   ∧ ⁄ ∪

12

###

A NEEBORT I.C.U. (A FLYING MACHINE)

I.C.U.s LIKE TRAKIRS ARE USED ALONE OR AS
PART OF A LARGER FLYING MACHINE.

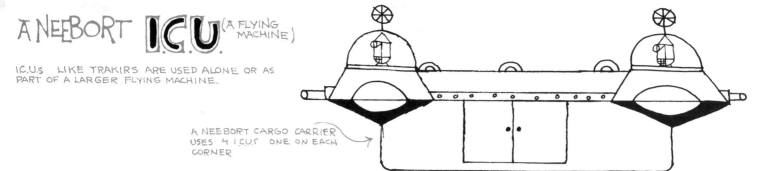

A NEEBORT CARGO CARRIER
USES 4 I.C.U.s ONE ON EACH
CORNER

SIDE VIEW

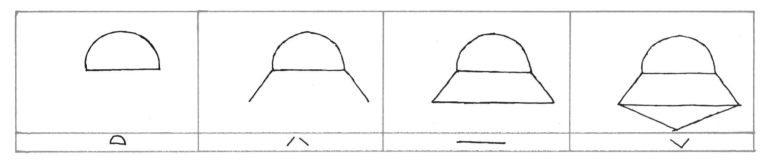

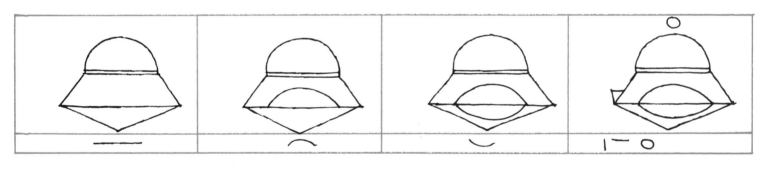

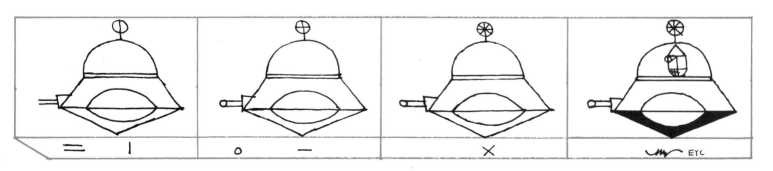

88

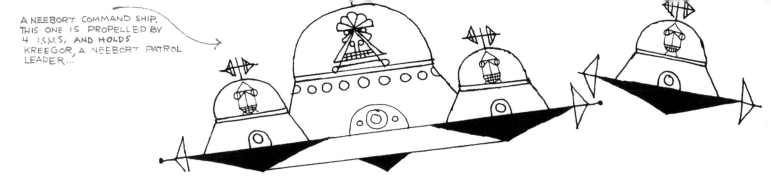

A NEEBORT COMMAND SHIP.
THIS ONE IS PROPELLED BY
4 I.C.U.S, AND HOLDS
KREEGOR, A NEEBORT PATROL
LEADER...

FRONT VIEW

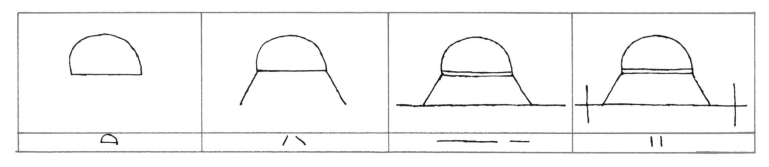

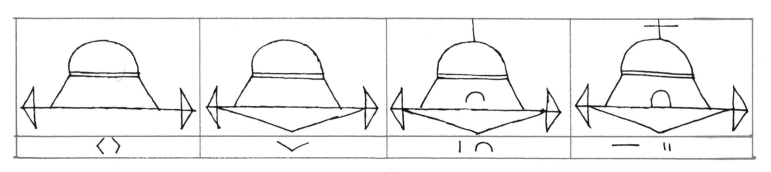

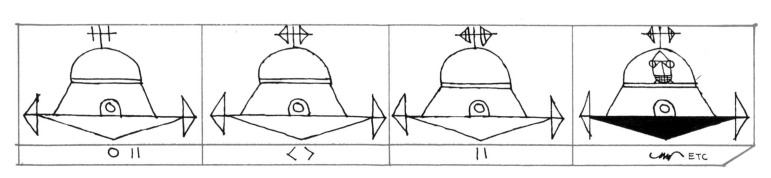

A NEEBORT
DRIM

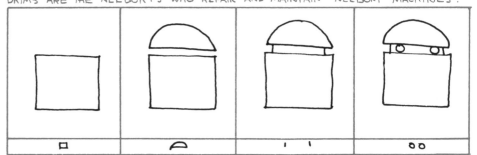

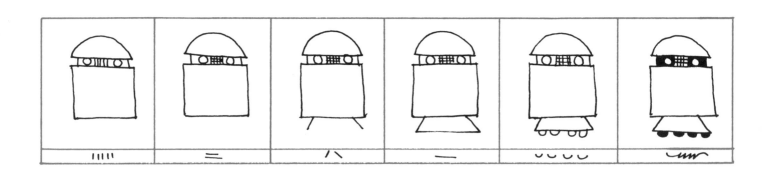

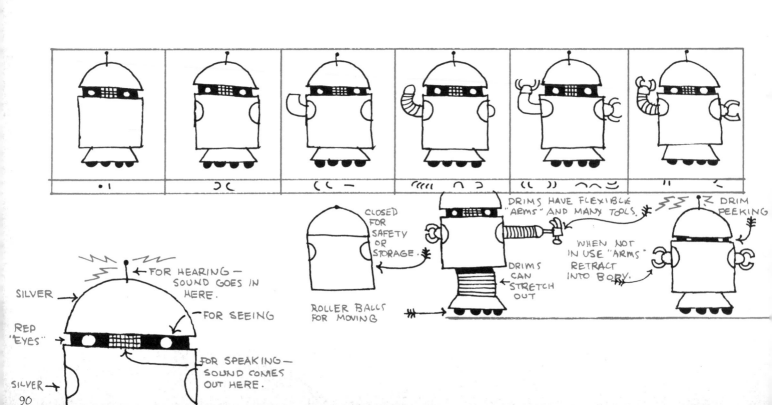

FOR HEARING — SOUND GOES IN HERE.

SILVER

FOR SEEING

RED "EYES"

FOR SPEAKING — SOUND COMES OUT HERE.

SILVER

CLOSED FOR SAFETY OR STORAGE.

DRIMS HAVE FLEXIBLE "ARMS" AND MANY TOOLS.

DRIM PEEKING

WHEN NOT IN USE "ARMS" RETRACT INTO BODY.

DRIMS CAN STRETCH OUT

ROLLER BALLS FOR MOVING

90

GINSFORTWOOZELLFIMMS

GINSFORTWOOZELLFIMMS ARE THE SMALL, PURPLE, FUZZY INHABITANTS OF "FRED" THE SMALLEST OF THE 7 MOONS OF ZORT. (ZORT IS IN THE BIG GREEN DRAWING BOOK) "FIMMS" HAVE NO BUILDINGS OR MECHANICAL DEVICES. THEY ARE NOMADIC AND SPEND MUCH OF THEIR TIME MOVING FROM PLACE TO PLACE ON THE DARK SIDE OF "FRED"

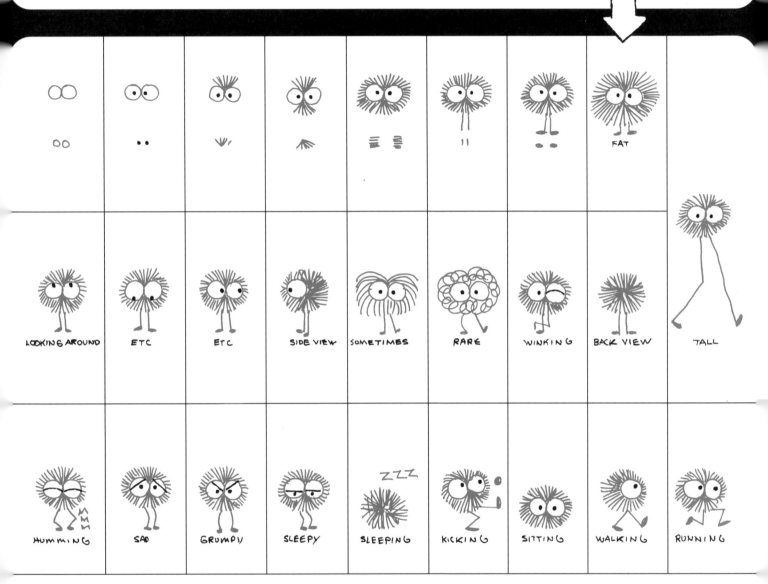

							FAT	
LOOKING AROUND	ETC	ETC	SIDE VIEW	SOMETIMES	RARE	WINKING	BACK VIEW	TALL
HUMMING	SAD	GRUMPY	SLEEPY	SLEEPING	KICKING	SITTING	WALKING	RUNNING

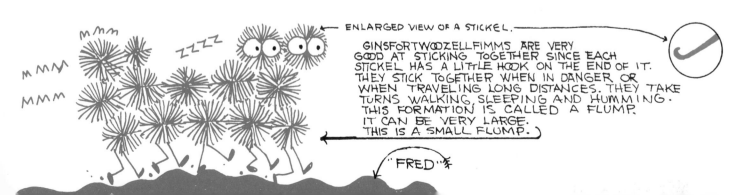

← ENLARGED VIEW OF A STICKEL. →

GINSFORTWOOZELLFIMMS ARE VERY GOOD AT STICKING TOGETHER SINCE EACH STICKEL HAS A LITTLE HOOK ON THE END OF IT. THEY STICK TOGETHER WHEN IN DANGER OR WHEN TRAVELING LONG DISTANCES. THEY TAKE TURNS WALKING, SLEEPING AND HUMMING. THIS FORMATION IS CALLED A FLUMP. IT CAN BE VERY LARGE. THIS IS A SMALL FLUMP.)

"FRED"

IF YOU FOUND SOME OF THE THINGS
IN THIS BOOK DIFFICULT TO DRAW THAT
IS BECAUSE SOME OF THE THINGS
IN THIS BOOK ARE DIFFICULT TO DRAW!

P.S.